# DETECTING GROWTH IN LANGUAGE

# Detecting Growth in Language

James Moffett

Boynton/Cook Publishers
HEINEMANN
Portsmouth, NH

Boynton/Cook Publishers, Inc.
A Subsidiary of Reed Publishing (USA) Inc.
361 Hanover Street
Portsmouth, NH 03801-3912
Offices and agents throughout the world

Library of Congress Cataloging-in-Publication Data

Moffett, James.
    Detecting growth in language / James Moffett.
      p.  cm.
    Includes bibliographical references.
    ISBN 0-86709-311-0
    1. Verbal learning—Evaluation.  2. Observation (Educational
method)  I. Title.
LB1059.M58  1992
428′.007  dc20                          92-18851
                                                  CIP

Printed in the United States of America
Printed on acid free paper
93 94 95 96   9 8 7 6 5 4 3 2

# Contents

Preface
vii

Alternatives to Standardized Testing
1

Matching Thought with Language
6

A Model of Mental Growth
8

Abstracting
11

Egocentricity
19

Explicit and Implicit
21

Both Modes of Knowing
24

Literal and Figurative
26

Ambiguity
30

## Naming
33

## Phrasing
40

## Stating
42

## Chaining
47

## Growth in Kinds of Discourse
56

## Conclusion
68

# Preface

This book is meant to help K–12 teachers assess verbal learning without external tests, by their own observations of learner activities and products. Now that the destructive nature of standardized tests has been well documented and recognized, especially in the individualized, interactive, and integrated programs advocated today, it becomes more important than ever for teachers to learn how to detect growth constantly as they witness students discussing or performing, read or hear their writing, watch or listen to their tapes, listen in on or sit in with groups, confer with individuals, and register individuals' patterns of choice in their activities, materials, and partners.

Since particular observations are infinite, all I can do here is suggest some general signs of growth to look for, or perhaps more accurately, some general ways of looking. I trust teachers' experience and native perception to fill in a great deal. The world of verbal learning is so large and intricate, however, that some developmentally significant ways of breaking it down and conceptualizing it should prove useful. To facilitate getting a mental handle on these ways of viewing growth, I have crystallized the discussion of each in a culminating sentence. So some two dozen of these boldfaced "growth sequences" periodically pull together the text.

Personal judgment may be subjective, as it has to be for assessing verbal growth, but it can be informed by teachers' cumulative experience with many different learners if thought about in the framework of ideas that follow here.

# Alternatives to Standardized Testing

External testing is no more necessary for learning in school than for learning out of school. It does not benefit those in the classroom, who can better assess in other ways. Standardized tests exist for people outside the classroom—for administrators and the public. All they do is compare one student or school or school system with another. This serves only to create mischief. Parents have a right to know how much schools are helping their children to learn, but they can ascertain this better from seeing their children's work and from talking with them. In good learning environments, students create a lot, which means that there is a lot for parents and administrators, as well as students and teachers, to see.

The way the public actually judges schools is by real performance in the world out of school, not by test scores, which mean little beyond academic walls. The most telling fact is that even students who once scored high and got high grades in, say, math or science remember too little to apply them later when they really need them. The complaints of employers and of graduates themselves tell us more than tests do. How well can the citizenry deal with ideas, communicate and collaborate with colleagues, make sense and use of texts, vote knowledgeably, and conceive solutions to problems?

Assessment experts, it's true, are working to make external evaluation more sophisticated than the crude multiple-choice, computer-scorable tests that have always shrunk the curriculum to fit themselves. Such experts repudiate standardized tests as we have known them and claim to be able to design testing activities that will do justice to any learning goal. But tests simple and cheap enough to permit comparison and to administer universally can never do justice to the depth and complexity of what educators are calling "higher literacy" and "critical and creative thinking" or "higher-order thinking." Furthermore, the more nearly such testing activities might succeed in assessing these desirable mental activities, the more nearly they would approximate the actual real-life performances themselves, in which case there's no need for special testing circumstances, since these performances can be observed where they authentically occur in and out of school.

In other words, if students are learning by doing, by practicing the target activities themselves, then anyone can evaluate by observing daily learning, because the learning and evaluating activities are one and the same. We can assess these activities by whatever means and standards we are all judging schools in society at large when we defend or indict them. This is ideal—if, again, the learning activities are the target activities themselves, not exercises alleged to lead to these goals. The most efficient education would never require of learners that they do anything especially for evaluation that they would not be doing anyway in order to learn. Furthermore, if special testing activity is required, it betrays the learning goals to the extent that it differs from them. And in order to accommodate the special conditions and costs of mass measurement, it must differ a great deal.

National assessment exists to embarrass schools into improvement by comparing scores. This assumes that dereliction is the problem and competition the answer. It's a crude, moralistic, negative approach. What evidence exists that the threat of getting beaten will spur and cure schools? The fact is that, as much as anything, this very authoritarian approach has demoralized teachers and principals, who simply never have had decision-making power commensurate with responsibility for the results, because tests and texts—the major determinants of curriculum—are usually selected over their heads, if not behind their backs. Perhaps the first reason schools have found improvement so difficult is that state and district legal requirements have built standardized tests into the curriculum and into textbook adoptions so that everybody has to teach to the tests and ignore both their personal expertise and the urging of their professional organizations.

The movement toward site management aims precisely to offset such top-down governance in the local districts by delegating decision-making powers to schools and neighborhoods. But the states and the federal government are neutralizing this movement by pushing national testing farther than it has ever gone before. The presidency and the governorships seem far less willing than the local districts to give power to the grassroots, perhaps because they don't have to live with, or can't see as well, the negative consequences of their efforts to control education through testing. Proponents of national assessment reiterate that participation in this competitive testing is voluntary, but they know perfectly well that when state and federal government throws its weight behind something, parents and communities will clamor to have it in *their* district. Actually, district and state school systems, like the individual students in them, differ far too much in far too many ways for scores to show who is and isn't doing a good job. The reasons for poor performance go far beyond mere reprehensible character. The whole idea of improving an institution by showing it up is negative and unfair. The legislators and other politicians who are adopting this get-tough policy to weed out incompetents are the very ones who have been, in effect, blocking educational improvement for decades already by decreeing assessment and procurement policies that conflict with what the best teachers are trying to do.

The official argument goes that if government permits site management and parental choice, then the educational results have to be measured against state and federal standards, to protect students from local ignorance or incompetence. But standards don't have to be set by *tests* and in fact *cannot* be set by tests, because standards are ideas of excellence that will always exceed what standardized instruments can afford to measure. Whether norm-referenced or criterion-referenced, furthermore, tests must allow most students to pass and therefore must anchor learning to *low* standards—an unnecessary self-contradiction caused by the insistence on competition. When an individual's progress is measured only against his or her past, standards do not have to be pegged low enough to accommodate masses. Comparing individuals against each other hampers everyone's progress by creating distracting self-concepts. Incessantly testing students, finally, amounts to putting them on probation throughout their youth. This creates chronic problems of low self-esteem and resentment toward schools, which should be there, after all, to serve them, not to shame and intimidate them.

How can we set standards without tests? Well, where do the criteria for tests come from if not from prior notions of what to look for in growth? It is these notions of growth in certain areas that provide standards. This is why I have emphasized in this book the *detecting* of growth in language—perceptive observation. It is an effort to describe signs of verbal growth that educators and parents may look for. Most of these kinds of growth, which I have tried to summarize periodically in italicized statements, could not be transformed into acceptable tests even were that a good idea.

Furthermore, some kinds of growth occur in the parts of discourse—like vocabulary or sentence structure—so that if tested in isolation, as is the traditional practice, would perpetuate exercises with them in isolation. Teaching to tests inevitably causes learning activities and conditions to resemble testing activities and conditions. But an observer can *notice* how a student is developing in the substructures of discourse without isolating these in the student's mind. In fact, such *in situ* observation allows the evaluator precisely to assess how a student is interplaying parts so as to create meaningful wholes. This holistic complexity of thought and speech is exactly what standardized testing will never measure.

Standardized tests rank students or schools but don't troubleshoot the problems of either individuals or institutions. Language educators need to learn what to look for so as to become more expert assessors and counselors in the learning process. In organic, student-centered language learning such as I have advocated else-where,* these two roles are synonymous. In order to guide students who are creating individual curricula while interacting with others, teachers have to evaluate constantly *and* have to teach students to do the same. All are charting past and future together on the basis of what previous activities have been worth and what is needed next. So both products and processes are examined all the time as mem-bers of reading and writing groups confer about texts, as writing is responded to and disseminated, as work folders fill up for perusal, and as texts are given rehearsed readings or otherwise performed live.

Discussions, improvisations, performances, writing workshops, and all sorts of projects can be frequently audiotaped and videotaped for several purposes at once—to allow participants to critique them-selves, to furnish material for teacher in-service discussions, to orient new students to these activities, and to show people outside the classroom what is going on inside. Many of these tapes may serve only temporarily and then be recorded over. Others may be saved along with selections from writing portfolios and other tangible prod-ucts to provide more lasting records. Doing both accommodates random, slice-of-life sampling of the whole curriculum and tracing of individual growth.

The point is to have plenty to look at so that any party can evaluate for any purpose. Observing processes as well as examining products permits realistic troubleshooting. Yet none of these activi-ties exists only for assessment; they are all learning processes. They are the target activities, the goals themselves of speaking, reading, writing, and thinking—of communicating, collaborating, decision-making, problem-solving, creating, and interpreting texts—not some exercises that are means only, alleged to eventuate sometime in these goals. What you're seeing is what you're getting.

Whether external testing simply disappears in the future, or whether it does indeed become identical with the learning activities that are the goals, perceptive observation will emerge as the central means of evaluating. Assessment reformers today base their claim to be able to measure higher thinking on what they call the three Ps—performances, portfolios, and projects. If they succeed, they will

---

* See *Student-Centered Language Arts, K–12,* James Moffett and Betty Jane Wagner, 4th edition, 1992 Boynton/Cook, Portsmouth, NH.

The chapter in it titled "Evaluating" also elaborates some of the issues and processes touched on in this book. Consult the chapters there on talking, improvising, performing, reading, and writing for specific things to look for in each of these activities.

be assessing in the routine classroom or workplace, not in special examination circumstances on rare occasions under conditions that permit numerical comparisons. The three Ps sound very good, if they are authentic language activities as practiced out of school. Performances, portfolios, and projects make up the kind of curriculum this book presupposes. Made available in some slice-of-life form to outsiders, they offer real alternatives to the old multiple-choice tests for external examination. In any case, they all depend on observers knowing how to look and how to think about what they see.

Freed from emceeing to observe in their own classroom, teachers can note personal traits and trends, comment on these as needed during conferences with students and parents, and write reports if required. When students are doing different things according to personal experience and choice, they look different because they create individual patterns that are far more distinctive than test-score profiles. Teachers know more surely how to coach, confer, and counsel toward improvement. The descriptions of growth spelled out in this book aim to help teachers think about what to look for.

Some of the most important signs of verbal growth are certain habits, attitudes, and feelings too obvious to dwell on here but necessary to reaffirm. Well-developing language learners will feel more at ease speaking, reading, and writing and will consequently increase their fluency and pleasure in these areas. By exploring what oracy and literacy can do, students will increasingly appreciate the multiple uses of language—to socialize, play, communicate, think, and create. By finding out the limitations of language, they will discriminate between occasions for words and occasions for silence. Confidence and curiosity increase. Choices multiply. Expression acquires verve and subtlety; interpretation, justness. Thinking broadens and deepens. Let's never forget to look for and register major human developments in expression and understanding as we break these down now into more specific things to detect.

# Matching Thought with Language

Any researcher who has tried to measure the effect of some teaching treatment on the growth of thought and speech knows what easy-scoring standardized tests ignore—that the presence or absence of a certain word or sentence structure does not necessarily indicate the presence or absence of certain thinking. The fact that people use the word *because* does not mean that they understand causality, for many small children use the word before they grasp the concept. The chief issue of assessment, in fact, is distinguishing between true growth and hollow verbalism.

The idea of causality, on the other hand, may be expressed in a discourse without the word *because* appearing in it. Concepts of relations especially are often conveyed "between the lines" by context. Juxtaposition and punctuation may convey the cause-and-effect relation: "He decided to leave; he knew they wanted to be alone." Omitting *because* makes the logic more implicit and gains the rhetorical advantage of understatement. If we were to measure growth by counting this author's logical conjunctions we would score her low because of her more sophisticated composing!

How do you offset this lack of one-to-one correlation between thought and language? On any one occasion you probably can't, because you don't have enough to go on. The smaller the sample of discourse, the greater the problem. *To judge language growth, you have to sample a learner's speech on many different occasions and make a composite judgment.*

Thought is invisible until it is translated into deeds or words. So while intellectual growth is more important, you most often have to detect it as manifested in language, because language incarnates thought. Since the language half is all we can see, we are much tempted to forget this invisible thought that it is being matched off with and even forget the whole process of matching. Too often teachers just focus on language forms as if these existed alone.

There are several reasons why thought and language cannot be matched off in predictable, standard ways. First of all, thought is more various; it is too big for words. The possibilities of what many individual human minds can conceive and combine are greater than the permutations possible with a single lexicon and grammar, although creative use of language, as in poetry, bends language to fit the mind.

Second, before less-developed learners have learned how to use all the resources of language, they must make shift to cast their thought into language by any means they can. So they will express their thinking in more ambiguous, less differentiated forms of language than if they knew how to employ all its resources.

Third, language does not exist merely to convey thought; besides its logical function it has a rhetorical function, to exert some kind of force on other people. So many of the choices speakers and writers make in composing aim to have an effect on other people, not just to express ideas. This justifies making an important distinction between *abstracting from* some raw source and *abstracting for* a certain audience.

Fourth, any shift of thought from one medium to another necessitates loss and slippage. Language can only do certain things. Like any medium, it has its limits. In fact, it is most likely true that language can never do complete justice to thought, especially the subtlest, deepest, most original thought. Mathematical language and symbolic logic were developed, in fact, to offset some of the logical deficiencies of ordinary language, as figurative language has served to symbolize "ineffable" feeling and intuition. Other media may be more successful sometimes in rendering certain kinds of nonlinear, nondiscursive perception. Language is a flexible mold, however, and growth consists of finding out just how much, and which kinds of, thought language can indeed render.

Finally, language arts are arts, and many of the options about how to put thought into speech are aesthetic choices for the sake of wit, play, economy, beauty, and so on. At the same time we put our thinking into words we are often also playing games with the medium somewhat for game's sake, as in painting, photography, dance, and other arts. Practitioners "make statements" in those media but also just use the media as wherewithal with which to compose form. We have to think of language as both means and end and look for growth at once in communication effectiveness and in word play.

# A Model of Mental Growth

Because teachers of composition and comprehension necessarily deal with the putting of thought into speech and the interpreting of speech into thought, they need a model of mental growth. They are not concerned with language alone. Problems of composition and comprehension have to be resolved *between* thought and speech as students try to match one with the other. The nature of language, moreover, influences thinking. The model of growth that educators choose makes a critical difference in how everyone involved thinks about learning.

The growth model assumed in much traditional schooling is based on nineteenth-century physics and the industrial assembly line. According to this mechanical model, an educated student is a "product" issuing from one end of a closed system into which he and some other inert materials were fed. Knowledge structures are assembled by putting small parts together to make subassemblies that are in turn put together to make the finished product. The upshot is that students can't see the woods for the trees. They are usually working on parts, without knowing why, and too seldom experience fully functioning communication in school. One falsity in this model is that in reality a child is more maker than made.

It's important, whatever the model, that it depict growth sequence as cumulative, not linear. Don't picture growth as a ladder or a series of stepping-stones, because these metaphors imply that learners leave behind old learning as they acquire new. Most learning is never shed but, rather, becomes assimilated or transformed into more advanced skills and knowledge. Imagine growth as a circle that becomes filled with more and more detailed and interfused figures.

Biology is the most appropriate field from which to draw a model of education, because mental growth parallels the growth of the total organism, in which it occurs. The best model of mental growth is the human embryo. It grows from a single cell to an extraordinarily intricate organism without ever being anything less than a whole and without ever functioning any other way than as a whole. A fertilized human egg is a human being before elaboration. What it is to become is already coded genetically within and will unfold through interaction with the environment. As the French expression says, "The more it changes the more it is the same thing"—that is, the more it fulfills what is has always been latently. It effects change by differentiating itself into limbs and organs, and it sustains itself across change by interrelating these parts by nerves and blood vessels as fast as they become articulated. The beauty of embryonic—and of mental—

development lies in the great biological principle of simultaneous *differentiation and integration.*

At birth the mind of a child is integral with the world, because it has never had to deal with the world. Just as the child's body partook of the mother's body its mind partook of surroundings with no consciousness of separation. Marvelous faculties of reason like classifying and inferring exist already in potential state but lie dormant, pending the environmental exchanges that will activate them.

Cut off from the mother the child begins to become conscious of itself. Thrust up against physical and social realities, the child begins to construct an ego to negotiate with the things and people it is now starting to feel separate from. Distinguishing one's organism from one's environment—perhaps the real trauma of birth—is the archetype of all differentiating. As it differentiates self from world, the child also differentiates the mind into thoughts that match the way the physical and social worlds are broken down. For safety and satisfaction, it has to learn to make distinctions to tell the difference between one thing and another. It learns to analyze, in other words, or, more accurately, its experience activates its inborn ability to analyze.

Humpty Dumpty's fall symbolizes this breakup of the egg's primal unity and simplicity into the inevitable differentiation an organism must undergo if it is to survive. The higher the animal the more its survival depends on acting differently toward different things—on flexibility—and hence the more it must differentiate its own insides into specialized parts. Growth means moving away from an initial lumping together, which in the mental realm some psychologists call global thinking. (Vestiges of it will hound students and teachers for years to come in the form of undiscriminated, undetailed, unrelated, unexplained ideas.)

Humpty Dumpty's problem is not that he broke himself down but that all the king's horses and all the king's men cannot put him back together again. The other half of growth is integration. As an *egg* Humpty Dumpty indeed cannot be put back together. An egg has to change into something else, and integrating new parts is actually *re*integrating. The differences emerging because of the breakdown must constantly be restructured. After a certain stage, nutrients no longer diffuse directly throughout protoplasm; gastrointestinal organs evolve to specialize in processing nutrients, and these organs must form a sequence among themselves, so that each does its job successively, and must form other appropriate relations with heart, lungs, brain, and so on to coordinate functions.

As the embryo must integrate the organs and vessels it articulates for fending and foraging in the environment outside the womb, the mind must organize the concepts and statements into which it is breaking thought down for matching it to material and social realities. The mind must synthesize parts into wholes at the same time it analyzes the whole into parts. Brain research suggests, in fact, that one reason for the brain having two hemispheres is so that it can specialize in both functions at once. Usually the left hemisphere (in most right-handed people) undertakes to analyze and the right to synthesize. The more differences the mind distinguishes, the more relating it must conceive in order to coordinate the parts as a whole. The mind must see the unlikeness of things existing in their unique state of concreteness and yet see likeness among things as reordered out of time and space into the abstract realm of thought. In its original global state of mind, the child is no more aware of similarity than of difference, because perception of one depends on perception of the other. Analysis and synthesis together create the complexity, the higher organization, that characterizes growth.

# Abstracting

Because the matching off of thought with the forms of language cannot be done on a one-to-one basis, an idea may be said many ways. The myriad options for matching thought with speech create, in fact, all the glories and problems of comprehension and composition. Working in the gap, then, between invisible thought and visible language, a teacher needs a concept applying equally to both. The concept of abstracting serves this purpose.

Abstracting is mentally mapping reality. It comprises two opposite processes, analysis and synthesis, working together simultaneously. By virtue of analysis, the mind is able to elaborate global wholes into their particulars. By virtue of synthesis, the mind is able to generalize otherwise disparate particulars into wholes. Elaboration emphasizes differences and leads into the world. From it we gain discrimination and detailed fidelity to reality. Generalization emphasizes similarity and leads into the mind. From it we gain increased scope and the power of mental relating. Neither can function without the other, for just as generalizing presupposes some prior breakdown into particulars from which generalities can be drawn, elaborating presupposes some prior generalities that can be broken down into particulars. Abstraction is a tension between the two processes. It binds mind to world.

This tension stretches across any effort to speak, listen, read, or write. In composition, teachers constantly urge students to be specific, to add concrete details to narrative and description or to give examples to illustrate their ideas in an essay. On the other hand, teachers push students to relate ideas to other ideas and to details, to give emphasis and unity, to "tie things together." All of these are classic issues in relating generality to instance so as to convey meaning. For comprehension, a reader must relate authors' little facts to their main points, draw conclusions from cues and clues, put examples and evidence in proper relation to statements they support, and "pull together" the various big and little things the author has said into an understanding that focuses on the general and subordinates the particular in the ratio an author intends.

## Generalizing

I'm using the term *abstract* here in its original meaning—to draw off. Don't be confused by the fact that the noun *abstraction* usually connotes only high-level generalization. I'm using the term here to denote the process of economically selecting and recasting traits of experience. When we speak of a trait, we mean that which is drawn off, again in accordance with the original meaning. The abstracter selects a trait that for one purpose or another he or she deems an important aspect of an object, event, scene, or experience.

Doing this presupposes some analysis: in order to select out *spotted* as a trait of some things, one first has to differentiate figures from backgrounds and spots from figures—that is, break down reality. A trait is drawn off to reduce and reorder the world. The speckles on fruit, the spots on some animals, the freckles on people, the dots on a blouse, the ground pattern of sunlight through leaves, knotholes in paneling, the dark and bright places in someone's "checkered career"—all become mentally digested in such a way that the spottedness of each dissociates itself from the concrete context in which it was embedded. This stripping off of local and detailed circumstances isolates the trait. Then, once singled out, a trait is ordered in the mind. It joins with the spottedness of the others to form a concept based on a common denominator, a vaguer image that can include sets of spots of different contexts, origins, purposes, colors, regularity. What is drawn from different sources is distilled to make a new mental entity. In this way, synthesis accompanies analysis.

Generalizing is a process of putting mind over matter. People don't draw off traits of things as they do broth from beef, of course, because both contains actual molecules of beef, whereas an abstraction can only *symbolize*—code from a physical to a mental medium—and hence must partake of mental qualities. The mind codes reality within its own medium of bioelectrical circuitry the way a television receiver recapitulates original action electronically on its screen—by forming itself to match the form it is simulating. Whereas the television receiver can recapitulate only temporal and spatial forms of matter in motion, the mind can make logical forms as well because it is a far more complex medium having ocular representation as only one of its submedia.

All that can be abstracted from something is *form*. The basic idea of informing is to put into form, and that's exactly what happens in matching experience with thought. Form is not a something but a relation—succession in time, direction and position in space, conjunction of circumstances or conditions. Relations are intangible, like mind itself. So thought can consist only of relating. Concepts result from sorting things into classes, and sorting is relating different things according to a common trait like spottedness. The traits themselves have to be formal in order to be drawn off—either an aspect of physical form such as spottedness or a relation such as that of owing in the concept of duty.

Abstracting spottedness shows at work the logical faculty responsible for generalization—*analogy*. (*Analogic* is thinking of things as like.) This is the same faculty responsible for metaphor. (The poet Gerard Manley Hopkins drew off spottedness in "Pied Beauty," which begins, "Glory be to God for dappled things. . . .") Generalizing is a form of thought that may take several language forms, as we shall show later; it is not just a class concept in noun or adjective form, as in the example above.

## Elaborating

To *elaborate* means to work out. Nothing can be elaborated that is not already contained as germ in the whole or generality to be elaborated. Elaboration is the flowering of an idea; seed differentiates into stem, root, leaves, and blossoms—all of which come from within. Elaboration is unfolding a given, whether the given is an object to be descriptively detailed, a summary of action to be filled in, a statement to be exemplified, or a premise from which corollaries are to be deduced. Buried in someone's use of *spotted* are concrete, remembered instances—fruit, fabric, or face—that he or she "has in mind" and could summon for elaboration. Elaborating particulars makes explicit ("unfolded") the referents of word, whereas generalizing leaves instances implicit, assumed. When the referent of a word is not a physical thing but an idea itself, then elaborating brings out the ramifications ("branchings"), the hidden implications.

Whatever the level, elaborating works by reversing generalization. Generalizing achieves scope by extending the referent over time and space—over all spotted things anywhere, any time. Elaborating achieves discrimination by narrowing the compass of time and space covered—down to some spotted animals at some times and places, for example, or one freckled child at one time and place. Elaborating localizes, puts things back into time and the concrete circumstances from which generalizing drew them. This leads to multiplicity, of course, for as generalizing subsumes many instances into one concept or statement—"uses up" raw material at a great rate, so to speak—specifying particulars restores original quantity, as well as quality, of experience.

Elaborating also turns up instances one had not thought of before. It is a tool for finding out fully what one means. Once armed, for example, with the concept of a spectrum, one could look for instances other than the orderly arrays of color shades and musical tones by which one may have first come to understand the concept and thus think of scaling metals by their degree of tensile strength or scaling people by their degree of patience. Or one might check how broadly a statement like "opposites attract" applies by thinking of as many instances of it in different domains as one can. So it is that elaboration leads back from mind to world in a reversal of analogy.

**Growth Sequence 1: Toward generalizing more broadly while elaborating more finely.**

This formulation aims directly at heading off the mistaken notion that either generality alone or detail alone is good of itself. An *overgeneralization* is a statement based on too few instances and hence lacks underpinning. Endless inventory of details, on the other hand, comes to no more than laundry and grocery lists until organized under some generality that relates particulars to each other and to elements in a discourse.

## The Dual function of abstracting

The function of abstracting is to enable individuals to match their minds to the world, on the one hand, and to fellow minds, on the other. *Abstracting from* experience makes information, to accommodate oneself to external realities. *Abstracting for* other people makes communication, to benefit from community. (One of the benefits is receiving other people's information.) The dual functions of informing oneself and communicating to others interact with each other, because the same abstracting apparatus is serving both. The habit of communicating information influences how people inform themselves. Thought is private and speech public, but constantly matching thought with speech inevitably causes thinking to become somewhat public and stereotyped. This influence can be reciprocal; thought can cause speaking to become somewhat private and original. The first statement of growth, along the logical dimension of *abstracting from,* should be paired off with the following statement of growth along the rhetorical dimension of *abstracting for.*

**Growth Sequence 2: Sending toward more general and more differentiated audiences.**

Together, the two very general kinds of growth frame the more specific sorts formulated throughout this book. The second one cannot be fully explained, however, before "Growth in Kinds of Discourse" later in this book.

## The Partialities of abstracting

The very function of abstracting biases it toward personal desire or public conventions (which represent communal desire). Mapping is always for a purpose, if only a playful one, and this purpose necessarily makes abstracting partial. Mental maps always specialize, like geographic maps, which may show mineral resources or air routes or ethnic distribution or temperature zones but never everything. No abstraction can render justice to all aspects of something, in its totality, because selective reduction is the point of abstracting. People can't deal with all aspects of all things. They have to choose traits according to their values. This is why content is a factor of intent. One trades a loss of reality for a gain in control, to get a mental handle on reality toward certain ends. Abstracting is decision-making. This is necessary for survival, but the great and haunting danger of boomeranging always remains: people may exclude from their maps aspects of reality more vital to them than those their desires or their society's conventions direct them to single out.

Abstractions can be true, then, only relative to some given value system and frame of reference guiding the selective reduction. They may be useful or beautiful but never true except in a partial way. Raw phenomena present themselves, and thought can only *re*present them in one or another biased way. This relativity unnerves many people, who simply cannot believe that the maps they and their fellows hold to be self-evident are not *the* maps. Or even if our own maps are not quite correct and complete, surely some maps somewhere are. But it is in the very nature and function of the abstracting process that it should fail to yield the absolute truth some part of a human being seems to hunger for.

Earlier eras made a distinction between human truth and divine truth. Religious beliefs aside, this distinction is necessary to remind us that no human being is desireless and unconditioned by society and that no human being has a vantage point of universal scope or impartiality. No matter how brilliant our mental faculties, our minds work in the service of mortals bound to a certain time and space and inheritance. This is why spiritual leaders have always said, "If you wish to know divine truths, you must link up with the divine, not seek to know in this way with the brain." To claim that one's utilitarian, scientific, and aesthetic statements about the world correctly and completely describe the world is to claim omniscience for reason.

Both mystics and scientists repudiate such intellectual arrogance. They agree that the world is too big for words, that if absolute knowledge comes, it comes by total illumination, not by putting back together with one faculty of reason what we have torn down with another, admirable as this dual process of synthesis and analysis is for its biological purpose. We cannot experience all of reality, cannot render all we experience into thought, and cannot render all we think into words. This may be why Hamlet tells Horatio that there are more things in heaven and earth than are dreamt of in philosophy.

**Growth Sequence 3: Toward increasing awareness that people create what they know and that this knowledge is partial.**

## Abstracting as composing and comprehending

Human beings are born composers. By drawing off traits of the world and rearranging them according to some mental order, people constantly compose reality, for composition literally means putting together, selecting, and arranging the elements of a medium. We put together our own world, more or less like other people's because of social influences and similarities in basic equipment, more or less different because of individual variations in background and heredity. Our mental maps are compositions.

The root idea of *comprehension* resembles remarkably that of composition, despite the fact that they are supposed to be opposing sender and receiver viewpoints. To comprehend means to take together. The difference between "put together" and "take together" is the difference between composing and comprehending. *Put* suggests that one has wider choice of what to select than *take,* which suggests that one is given a previously selected set of things from which to abstract for some purpose. This is in fact exactly the case in reading, for example, where one must make sense of someone else's writing. Writers have a similar problem, however; they have to make sense not of something someone else has abstracted, but of the matter they confront. If people run up against either a text or an experience that they cannot fit into their previous mental maps, they say they don't know what "to make of it." Similarly, we say of speakers or writers, "They don't make sense." The common idea that people *make* sense, create meaning, seems to acknowledge that whether composing something themselves or comprehending someone else's composition, people are in the same basic position. Whether faced with physical events or a book, one has to interpret. Interpreting is one kind of abstracting. Within this similarity of *making* sense, then, composing and comprehending differ in whether one is abstracting from raw reality or from another's abstraction of it. Listening or reading is digesting someone else's digestion. This is a difference in the *level* at which one is abstracting.

## Levels of abstraction

Actually, no reality is truly raw by the time people become conscious of it. All that the nervous system can do is simulate in the medium of the body those phenomena it registers. A retinal image, for example, is the body's equivalent of the artist's conception. So the sensory impressions from which people abstract concepts are themselves abstractions. There are higher and lower orders of abstraction within both perception and conception, as we will explain further on. Moreover, as we just said, people make some of their information by comprehending other people's compositions in various media—that is, by abstracting from others' abstractions. Any such successive abstracting creates higher levels from lower ones. People not only make the reality they know, they make it by abstracting higher abstractions from lower ones. Knowledge-making is hierarchical.

Processing matter into mind comprises several stages that relate to degrees of growth. The nervous system codes external reality from the outside in, first with the muscles or motor apparatus, then with the senses, then with memory, and finally with reason. Stages may be bypassed, as when we learn about something from pictures only or as when we read about something, but when we abstract for ourselves from the ground up, each of these four knowledge-making faculties abstracts from the abstractions created by the faculties below. Reason doesn't go directly to work on raw external reality; it operates on what the senses represent to it of external reality, most of which has been filed away in the memory. And memory depends completely on sensory reports for the material it files away. Sensory perception abstracts information from external reality on the basis of body placement, position, movement, the quality of the sense organs, and interaction with environmental objects. What we see is limited to where the body takes the head and which way the head directs the eyes, so that abstracting begins with the organism's own selective action. (Moreover, some sensors report what is going on just within the body itself.)

It is imperative, however, to understand the two-way nature of abstracting. The case is not that reason is the victim of wayward sensorimotor apparatus and memory. To a point it is fair to say that the muscles, the senses, and the memory have minds of their own, because each is a specialized part made to function in a certain way, and the information created by each is unique. But the overriding fact is that these components are told what to report on. The mind executes the orders of the will and the emotions by *organiz*ing all functions around these orders. Orders are to screen reality according to declared priorities. So the muscles, senses, memory, and reason all abstract under constraints imposed from above at the same time that they report upward. This compares to personnel at different echelons of a social organization sending reports to their superiors about what their superiors want to be informed of, not just about anything they might take it into their heads to say. Each echelon gives form to what it receives according to both its own form and the shaping directions it operates under.

The report at each echelon summarizes the reports submitted to it from echelons below, in pyramidal fashion, so that information becomes more reductive and further removed from original sources the higher it goes. The final report placed on the president's desk or sent to trustees or shareholders has the virtue of being pertinent to what they want most to know about, but the successive abstractions risk loss of fidelity to the original external reality. More and more the organism or organization is processing previous processing. This is how the abstracting *for* cannot in practice be separated from abstracting *from,* and this principle of mind over matter reaches down to the very lowest level of abstracting.

# Egocentricity

For undeveloped speakers, the way speech comes out seems to be the only way the ideas could have been cast into language. Indeed, they don't really distinguish thought from speech at all and attribute to words a kind of magical absoluteness. Unable to envision alternatives, they cannot appreciate what is artful and cannot know how some utterance that does not work could have been better.

To be egocentric is to assume too much. Egocentricity is the main cause of communication difficulties in comprehending and composing. People assume at first that minds match, that other people see the world as they do, think about it the same way, mean the same thing when they use the same words, and fill in the gaps of language as they do. Thinking that something couldn't be any other way is the very essence of egocentricity. Writers are sure that what they write can be taken only one way, and readers are sure they understand the text in the only way it can be understood. The assumptions, furthermore, are hidden. People don't know what it is they don't know. They overcome egocentricity only very slowly, and so it is developmental, a lifelong process requiring much verbal and social experience to discover that minds do not match as specifically as we thought but rather have to be matched in many particulars.

Examples of egocentricity in reading are omitting cues to meaning, skewing the selection of points or details, "reading in" what is not there, and failing to get in the author's point of view to follow his or her intent. Examples in writing are missing punctuation, "poor transitions," "illogicality," "lack of focus," "incoherence," overexplaining or underexplaining, and "weak organization." In other words, take almost any serious problem that teachers agree occurs universally in comprehension and composition and you will find, if you examine it closely, that it is caused by unawareness of one's limited point of view. One way to put the matter is that successful readers must be able to role-play the author if they are to comprehend what the author is trying to say and how he or she is going about it. Conversely, authors must role-play ("allow for") their audience.

Egocentricity is the smallest of several concentric circles that fence in our individual minds. We are also ethnocentric—inclined to view life from within a set of ethnic, racial, cultural, and linguistic assumptions that are hard for us to see because, like our private assumptions, they are taken for granted. We can "be subjective" collectively, sharing with some people a mental set not shared by people outside our group. Individuals differ in their thought and perception and values partly just as a result of being born into different groups. Every culture and every language are biased. Although some aspects of all languages are universal, the assumptions built into each language are not the same for all, and often the differences can be startling.

We are also geocentric, sexcentric, and so on. Most of humanity's breakthroughs in thinking are *removals* of ideas—unthinking something that was not so or was partial. As children grow they become increasingly aware of cognitive options in how things can be thought about. More and more they unthink ideas they took for granted. This is the real meaning of *open minded.* It does not deprive thinkers of a position. The key, again, is awareness. They know where they stand. This awareness not only liberates their minds, it makes it possible for them to use language judiciously.

**Growth Sequence 4: Toward increasing awareness that meaning resides in minds, not in words, and that different people may see the same things differently, verbalize the same ideas differently, and interpret the same words differently.**

# Explicit and Implicit

Listeners or readers who don't understand a communication don't know if the failure is theirs or the sender's. If the communication is oral, however, sender and receiver can talk together and find out, in effect, whose hidden assumptions impede the message. But if the communication is written, the reader cannot let the author know what he doesn't understand so that the author can cast her ideas another way or make more explicit her intent and content. Such a situation puts a premium on the sender's judging right *the first time* around. She has to be aware enough of her possible egocentricity to *predict* the problems a reader may have in understanding what she's trying to say. It puts a premium on the reader's getting the meaning *on one attempt* by the author.

Both efforts require awareness of similarity and difference between sender and receiver. If the receiver knew everything the sender plans to tell him, the communication wouldn't be needed in the first place. So some discrepancy must be assumed. Yet both have to assume they already share a great deal, or else the author would have to fill in a whole culture's worth of background before she could begin to make her particular points. Here's the crux of the verbalization issues. How much detail people need to make explicit in communicating depends on how much they can assume a receiver shares with them certain factual knowledge, frameworks of understanding, and values. The less the difference between the speaker and listener, the less detail is needed. Tolstoy said that lovers talk in mumbled fragments because they know so well already what's on each other's mind that they need to convey very little.

One of the indications of maturity is the ability of a speaker to predict what different receivers will need to have made explicit for them and what they will understand without elaboration. The small child will expect you to know who Charlie is when he refers to him, whereas an older person will throw in an appositive like "Charlie, my wife's brother, . . ." This is how sentence structure and other language forms grow as a result of growth in awareness of differences. For their part, receivers must anticipate that some parts of the communication are omitted and assumed, and they must be prepared to fill them in.

An eighteen-month-old child may have to use the single word "Juice" to say "Give me some juice," "Is that my juice?" or "I'm drinking juice." An adult too may employ "Juice" as a whole utterance, in response to the question, for example, "What are you going to serve to drink?" His answer is really, "I am going to serve juice."

For both infant and adult in these cases, the subject and the predicate of the unfinished sentence are implied and have to be "understood." The adult's "Juice" can indeed be understood from the context the conversation creates, but the context for the infants' "Juice" resides only in his mind, and his utterance remains obscure or ambiguous unless the listener can infer his meaning from the context of the child's action toward the juice as he speaks.

The adult could, if pressed, replace "Juice" with the whole statement it stands for, but the infant has no choice, because (1) he cannot yet sort out his global states of mind into parts that fit the parts of speech used to make sentences, (2) he has not yet figured out the different parts of speech and how to put them together to make statements, and (3) he is unaware of the ambiguity and of the listener's need for elaboration. It is likely that all three grow along together, if unevenly, and that any differentiating of one sort—parts of thought, parts of speech, or speaker from listener—will bring along differentiating of another.

In verbalizing her experience for a listener, a speaker is making explicit for herself as well as her listener what until then was a cloudy impression made up of many details she had not singled out in her mind. In uttering the experience she differentiates it into aspects that *fit language*—subjects, actions, objects, time, place, manner, and so on. Eventually she becomes more expert at expressing similar experiences, because language breaks experience down into only so many classes and relations, but even as a very mature speaker later in life she will have trouble making some new experiences explicit because she has not yet tried to parcel them into language. Experience that is especially hard to shape into language may get ignored even by the experiencer, since not making it explicit for others in speech may cause her to remain unaware of it also. So growth in explicitness is relative to the nature of the experience—the less common, the harder to verbalize.

All this is not to say that making thought explicit is always and automatically a good thing. In the first place, as I said, it is impossible in any one communication situation to make *everything* explicit. Some things must be assumed—either some frameworks, on the one hand, or some details, on the other. The receivers have to draw some conclusions and supply some illustrations themselves. Furthermore, besides being unavoidable to some degree, implicitness is the main mode of the highest language expression—literature. So in an exact parallel to the simultaneous growth toward generalization and elaboration, people develop at once along the reversed directions of explicitness and implicitness.

**Growth Sequence 5: Toward increasingly sensitive judgment about when explicitness or implicitness is more appropriate in composing and comprehending.**

# Both Modes of Knowing

There is another reason why growth must be toward greater implicitness as well as explicitness, and this may be the real reason for literature. Language must do justice to the two main ways by which, we said earlier, the hemispheres of the brain abstract experience. French, German, and other languages have two different verbs for these two modes of knowing (*savoir* and *connaître, wissen* and *können*), so well were they recognized centuries before modern brain research—intuitively at least! The one associated with the analytic hemisphere is the intellect, and the one associated with the synthesizing hemisphere is intuition. Interestingly, all cultures consider intuitive knowing "direct." Intellect emphasizes parts and differences; intuition, wholes and similarities.

The analytic hemisphere sequences separate items in linear, cumulative fashion, moving in a time progression. It is digital and specializes in seriation. It is called the verbal hemisphere because language too is linear and analytic and seems to be essentially controlled by this half of the brain. But the two halves do work in tandem, after all, so that verbalization is significantly influenced by the mode of operation of the synthesizing hemisphere, even though that half is regarded as nonverbal.

The synthesizing hemisphere processes items simultaneously instead of sequentially and therefore is associated with space rather than time. It is analogical and specializes in classification. In holistic fashion, it fuses information coming from different sources at the same time. Because of its spatial orienting, it is associated with arts, sports, and crafts. It works by collecting diverse items together into a constellation based on some intuition of affinity among them. It is metaphorical. It links experience *implicitly,* whereas the analytic hemisphere names and states explicitly.

If language is to render thought effectively, it must somehow capture both of these modes of knowing—even though its own functioning is characterized by the analytic/linear hemisphere. Since growth occurs in both modes, and since language tries to do justice to both, we have to look at how it pulls off this feat.

To be explicit is to verbalize, to put into words rather than merely to imply. This difference between what is actually stated and what is left unstated strikes at the heart of our matter here, the rendering of thought into speech. The working of the analytic hemisphere naturally tends to make thought explicit in language, because it breaks thinking down into the kinds of items and relations that characterize language—the grammatical parts of speech, the types of sentence structures, and the kinds of discourse. Indeed, the fact that only humans have specialized hemispheres has prompted a hypothesis that specialization evolved to facilitate speech. But how does language render the thought that characterizes the synthesizing hemisphere?

# Literal and Figurative

*Literal* refers to letters, *figurative* to figures of speech. When a gardener talks about how to prune roses, he speaks literally in using their name; he doesn't, like a poet, refer to roses only as a way of referring to love or intellectual beauty or the house of Tudor. The difference here is between single and multiple levels of meaning. Gardeners, like scientists, don't intend for *the referent to refer in turn* to something else. They mean nothing but a rose. Wishing to strip the poor overloaded rose of all its culturally accumulated burden of symbolism, Gertrude Stein said, somewhat testily perhaps in her rebellion against the philosophical poetry of the preceding generations, "A rose is a rose is a rose."

A word used literally denotes one and only one thing. If the word normally has several possible meanings, like the word *interest,* only one of those is intended. Used figuratively, a word connotes more than its common meaning or any one of its meanings alone. It implies more than it says. So to speak literally is to be more explicit, to narrow down meaning precisely, whereas to speak figuratively is to refer simultaneously to several things at once. *Equivocal* means exactly this (equivocal implying several-voiced), and the useful counterterm is *univocal* (single-voiced). James Joyce tried to create a whole language of words such as "gracehoper" that would have meaning at two or more levels. But ordinary language is virtually like this, since the etymology of most words shows that they have or had a primal, concrete meaning upon which the more familiar one is overlaid. In this way Joyce's language is like any other, but his also makes new connections among things as original metaphor always does. The root meaning of *metaphor* itself, for example, is to carry over.

Any metaphor links together two otherwise unconnected items. A person who speaks of a politician put at bay is referring by one term to two referents—some politician and some game animal that hunting hounds have closed in on and backed into an impasse. The term bridges two domains, synthesizes two items within some similarity. The receivers have to fill in some of the meaning from their own imaginations, because metaphors work implicitly. They must decide for themselves how far the comparison goes—perhaps even of what the comparison consists. There isn't one term for each referent but one term for both. That is how metaphors operate implicitly. The same concepts that are serially conveyed over time, one concept per word in literal usage, can be conveyed in a single figure of speech, metaphor, or representative token. The term *condensation* has been used to denote this sort of multilevel expression when it occurs in dreams. It applies equally well to figurative language, which *compresses several levels of thought into one language term.*

The same is true for the symbolic figures and actions abounding in folk literature, novels, and other imaginative stories. Ostensibly, *Beowulf* or *Moby Dick* or *Alice in Wonderland* has a single level of meaning, since only one thread of language spins out the cumulative sequence, and, taken at face value, these works are productions of the analytic hemisphere. Items and actions are explicitly designated, and the subject matter is broken down and spread over parts of speech and sentence structures that dutifully dole it out according to conventional public categories. But what an extraordinary, original rendering of experience and thought! The authors have *embodied* their ideas in representative figures and deeds that stand for more than themselves. So a whale and a sea chase manage to carry along several levels of meaning simultaneously—psychological, physical, sociological, anthropological, theological—in exactly the way that the synthesizing hemisphere asserts simultaneously and implicitly a complex of different things.

The verbal work does not have to be fictional, however. Most case histories are cases because the central figure or group or experience is *typical,* that is, acts not just as referent of the words but refers in turn to other things in the common experience of reader and writer. A token represents a type, so that referring to the token automatically refers to the type as well and hence to all the other members of it. For example, Melville's white whale is a symbol. What is said about it at one level applies to other levels in the story as well.

This amounts to compressing generality and illustration into one entity. To the extent that it is literal, standing only for itself, a case at hand is only an instance that might be used to illustrate a general point; but to the extent that it is figurative, standing for others of a class, the case states a generality and illustrates it at once, though the generality, like the symbolism of the white whale, may never be stated *in so many words.* Literal discourse works by *embedding* generalities as particular sentences, strategically positioned in a discourse, which are supported by examples separately stated. Figurative discourse works by *embodying* generalities throughout the whole in recurring tokens invested with extra meaning by a web of suggestive details.

Compare literal meaning to melody, in which one note at a time is struck sequentially, and figurative meaning to chords, in which several related notes are struck simultaneously. Figurative language has overtones and undertones because several things are being referred to *at once.* Neither use of language is good or bad but has its own function. Both must be practiced. When people speak literally, they take one meaning at a time and build some kind of linear, cumulative abstraction, the way they play a tune by sounding one note at a time. When people speak figuratively, they express several meanings together in a complex, the way they strike a chord.

Literal language parcels out thought into speech in such a way that each concept is assigned its own term. In making language commensurate with the thought it conveys, this mode takes longer and allows only one connection among concepts at a time but makes each concept stand out separately, as the notes do in a melody. Figurative language is more economical and emphasizes the kinship and the totality of the concepts considered at once but makes it hard to single out any one of them from the rest and to make explicit what the relations are among them. A chord is like a fundamental, general idea in that it contains many possible melodies, as an idea contains implications and ramifications that can be spun out separately. Each melody is an elaboration of a chord, and each chord is a complex of potential melodies united by some intuition of vibrational affinity. Such is the *resonance* of the experiences Moby Dick stands for.

Figurative use of language answers the question how language can manage to serve at once both modes of knowing though controlled itself essentially by the linear/analytic hemisphere. The secret seems to lie in a certain kind of close collaboration between halves: intuition synthesizes experience into metaphorical complexes and feeds them in explicit sequences. It's as if the analogical half, specializing in classification, makes up the collections or categories of experiences, while the digital half, specializing in seriation, names and chains these categories. The digital half processes literal and figurative names the same way, so that it can be fooled if the names are equivocal, not univocal. It is not concerned with what isn't said.

The analogical halves of sender and receiver have to conspire, in a sense, to put in and take out of the words what isn't said. This is why shared experience must be assumed. Assuming is dangerous, as we have implied, but the only alternative is to limit communication to one mode of knowing. At any rate, communicating the analogical perceptions through the digital mode is like sending a coded message by means of an unwitting messenger.

The linear half performs its work not on raw material but on material as abstracted already by the holistic half. This same coordination occurs in music when a melody is played out a note at a time as the harmony sounds with and includes these notes in chord *progressions,* which are sequenced complexes. (See Figure 1.)

**Figure 1**
The Specialized Halves of the Brain in Most Right-handed People

| LEFT HEMISPHERE | RIGHT HEMISPHERE |
| --- | --- |
| Intellectual | Intuitive |
| Analytic | Synthetic |
| Linear | Holistic |
| Verbal | Nonverbal |
| Sequential | Simultaneous |
| Temporal | Spatial |
| Digital | Analogical |
| Explicit | Implicit |
| Literal | Metaphorical |

Source: This table owes a lot to Robert Ornstein, *The Psychology of Con-sciousness,* 1977, New York: Harcourt Brace Jovanovich. This is a good book for the layperson and one that I recommend highly, but research in hemi-sphericity evolves rapidly. For updating see *Brain/Mind Bulletin,* P. O. Box 42211, Los Angeles, CA 90042.

# Ambiguity

Language loaded with multiple meaning is called *ambiguous,* a term like *equivocal* that more often than not suggests that the sender has failed to communicate clearly by not stipulating which of several possible meanings is the one the receiver should select. But it is equally clear that the story of Moby Dick is meant to be ambiguous and that when people speak of the "rich meaning" of much great literature they are praising its ambiguity. Puns and double-entendres are *supposed* to mean more than one thing. So whether ambiguity is desirable or not depends on whether it is intended or not and whether, if intended, it is appropriate or not. Who wants manuals for Strategic Air Command missions to be rich in ambiguity? Most composing problems stem from unintended ambiguity, stemming in turn from egocentricity. Most comprehending problems result from not expecting ambiguity in what one is hearing or reading, so that one is misled by others' unintended ambiguity or interprets figurative language literally.

**Growth Sequence 6: Toward increasing ability to verbalize literally, when unintended and pointless ambiguity will otherwise result, and to verbalize figuratively when multiple meaning is desirable.**

To grow is to become aware of ambiguity, whether engendered by design or by default. This awareness relates directly to the decline of egocentricity, since it is egocentricity that prevents the learner from knowing whether a verbalization is ambiguous. As composers we must know what we have not made explicit that our receiver needs to know. As comprehenders, we must know when a talk or text should be taken literally and when it aims for multileveled meaning of metaphor and pun and representative token. Further, we need to understand when a speaker or writer is creating unintended ambiguity through egocentricity. What teachers call "literal-minded" is a tendency to interpret all discourse on a single level even when the language is figurative and the discourse allegoric or symbolic. Likewise, some learners seem tone-deaf or insensitive to connotations and overtones, the subtler effects of holistic simultaneity, for the similar reason that they are overfastened in the linear, literal, denotative mode.

This kind of incapacity sounds suspiciously school-induced, however, rather than native to childhood, because children are coming from a global state of mind in which the synthesizing mode is most natural, as we can see from their love of far-fetched and highly symbolic stories in which "incongruity" is permitted. Since they can't be identifying with such unrealistic figures and events, they must be attached to what those things represent. Teachers often err in forcing students to paraphrase deliberately ambiguous works in an unambiguous, literal statement—an endeavor that is bound to fail, that makes students detest literature, because it makes them look stupid and that thwarts the whole point of such works, which is to communicate to the analogical hemisphere of the mind.

Tolerating ambiguity is a mark of maturity, for it is often useful and, even when not, must be expected and dealt with. There is no way to avoid it, but as people grow they learn increasingly how to exploit it when they want and minimize it when they want. But literal-minded people fear ambiguity. They do not want to believe that things may not be what they seem. They insist rigidly on literal meanings in language as they do on physical appearance in life. The absurd lengths to which some English teachers push symbol-chasing and the hunt for hidden meanings make such people feel justified in reading both books and reality as flat and single-leveled. If not pushed constantly to translate figurative into literal, they would respond fearlessly to ambiguity and thus handle it appropriately. So growth here amounts to really undoing a culturally induced problem, the child certainly not being born to reject metaphor.

Many children have experienced disturbingly mixed messages from parents or other adults and fear plural meanings because these have been contradictory. Beaming contradictory messages to some-one at the same time places the receiver in a double bind—unless that person can become aware that precisely that is happening to him. Classically, a child hears others say one thing and sees them do another, or say with words something that their voice or gesture contradicts. If he responds to the signal in one channel, he is wrong by the other. The underdeveloped person just tunes out altogether.

Such a student misses both metaphor and irony. Irony scares him, because it is saying the opposite of what you mean in order to say better what you do mean. An A. E. Housman poem about death skips nimbly along in a lively meter. When you know this is deliberate and can accept multiple signals for their richness, you appreciate this consonance between form and content under the apparent dissonance. Understanding the reason for the ambiguity or dissonance—the confusion or the artfulness of other people, as the case may be—releases the fearful person from the double bind. This requires "standing in the other's shoes." Learners need to know that they can respond to mixed signals at once and don't have to select only one to respond to. Only awareness and a larger perspective will permit them to make some whole in their minds of the mixed signals. Then they can respond to the whole at once.

**Growth Sequence 7: Toward increasing ability to attune to multiple meaning levels in discourse and to discriminate between egocentric and intended ambiguity in messages one receives.**

Next let's look at growth more specifically in successively larger units of discourse—the word, the phrase, the clause, the sentence, the paragraph, and the organization.

The main way a learner grows verbally is toward increasing the number of options about how to compose thought into language and how to interpret language into thought. This enables learners to send and receive messages with people increasingly different and distant from themselves. These options are played in four main language actions—the naming, phrasing, stating, and chaining of ideas. That is, individual words are assigned to stand for concepts; concepts are elaborated by clustering words into phrases; the clusters are related by predicates to make clauses; the clauses are related in turn by logical connectives; and sentences are organized into sequences and patterns to make whole discourses. For developed speakers choices exist about how to name, phrase, state, and chain their own ideas, and about how to interpret the way others have named, phrased, stated, and chained their ideas. Of course, they're making these choices in context, holistically, not one at a time, discontinuously, as we will examine them next.

# Naming

Words stand for concepts, and concepts grow as youngsters grow. Learning new words and learning new meanings for old words go together. The size of a person's vocabulary may well indicate growth, but we cannot take quantity at face value. Everything depends on how maturely learners understand a word. They can acquire vocabulary only as they can grasp the concepts, and this understanding will depend on worldly experience and logical development.

As things in the environment become increasingly singled out for learners by seeing other people behave toward them and pointing them out, by physically engaging with them, or by comparing them by means of their own sensorimotor equipment, they form increasingly separated concepts of these things. Finer conceptualizing of anything—colors, musical tones, feelings, political positions—depends partly on experience in the area of the particular subject matter (Eskimos distinguish more kinds of snow than people usually do in temperate climates) and partly on the sensitivity of a person's overall mental and physical development. Differentiating the environment, differentiating concepts, and differentiating names all influence each other.

Concepts develop in the same direction as the rest of mental growth—toward broader generalization and finer elaboration. Concepts will extend further over time and space. Children may at first understand the concept of duty as household or classroom chores, then perhaps as some local allegiance or patriotism, then much later as giving every part of creation its due. Similarly, they will gradually expand the concept of trading baseball pictures with friends to bartering among tribes and to the complex of tariffs and balance of payments that comprise international trade.

At the same time, the number of members in a class concept swells, spreading also over time and space, because learners discover from refining their discrimination that these classes have subclasses. At first, the concept of watergoing vessels is limited to the few boats a person has had experience with—a rowboat with outboard motor, let's say, a simple sailboat, and pictures of ocean liners. The concept is vague and global, failing to distinguish less visible traits such as the purpose or the power source and not even distinguishing much about silhouette and structure. Gradually the learner distinguishes yacht from tanker, motor-powered from sail-powered, river-plying from ocean-going, and so on. Discriminating catamaran from schooner from clipper makes one realize that a whole subclass of sailing boats exists having in turn its own membership of subclasses and unique instances.

A less physical concept may not break down into such a definite and systematic branching of particulars but may nevertheless comprise specialized submeanings, as the general concept of duty eventually comprises, as one grows, the concept of a customs tax. As with all abstracting, the combined power of generalizing and elaborating creates hierarchical knowledge of increasing internal complexity.

**Growth Sequence 8: Toward concepts of broader applicability, of larger membership, and of greater internal complexity of subclasses.**

In some cases children learn a more general word first, and in some cases a more specific. Surely most children learn *boat* before *dinghy* and call every water-navigating vessel a boat. Many children call every quadruped *dog* at first, whether the animal is a horse, goat, or tiger. By contrast with *boat, dog* represents the case of learning first the more concrete word and moving upward to the more abstract (*quadruped,* or perhaps *mammal*). How specific or general are the words children first learn depends on what is most practical, so that you can expect vocabulary to begin with both concrete and abstract words. What you can count on for consistency is that both will be somewhat misused until the concept fills out in the other direction. Calling all quadrupeds *dog* is overgeneralizing the word, which designates only some quadrupeds, and calling all water-navigating vessels *boat* is overconcretizing (since for any one instance that a person has in mind, a more specific word exists).

**Growth Sequence 9: Toward vocabulary that more precisely fits the generality level of the concept the user actually has in mind.**

## Naming by parts of speech

The most explicit way to verbalize a concept is to name it with a word especially assigned to it. If a concept is conventional enough to be assigned its own word, and if the speaker knows that word, she may affix the word to the concept. Tradition recognizes nine kinds of words, the grammatical parts of speech—nouns, verbs, adjectives, adverbs, pronouns, articles or determiners, prepositions, conjunctions, and interjections (the last of which we will not consider, since they do not name things but vent feeling). A crude sort of growth order may be plotted among these parts of speech, of some value in the early years, but longer-range growth centers on *alternatives* about how to name things. Naming with single words is itself only one alternative.

Concepts of objects are easier than concepts of relations, and concepts of time-space relations are easier than concepts of logical relations. Because some parts of speech name one of these sorts of concepts and some another, parts of speech vary in degree of learning difficulty. So growth in use of the different parts of speech is linked with abstractive growth of concepts. The hardest parts of speech of all are those that do not refer to the subject matter but refer rather to the communication about the subject matter. Let's call this communicating about the communication itself *meta*-communication, *meta* meaning on a higher plane. Whatever is meta in respect to something else governs it and is necessarily more abstract and hence more difficult.

*Varying abstractive difficulty*   Proper nouns, common nouns, and pronouns represent a definite abstraction hierarchy corresponding to a growth sequence in the preschool years. A proper noun like *Wyoming* refers to only one particular item—something literally in a class by itself. A common noun like *state* refers to a whole class of like items, each of which alone might, like Wyoming, have a proper name. Children find proper nouns easier to learn because a singular referent requires little abstracting and because virtually no choice exists for how to refer.

One alternative does exist always, however, for proper nouns as well as for common nouns: a speaker may substitute a pronoun for the original noun and refer to Wyoming, for example as "it" or Mommy as "she." Pronouns are comparatively sophisticated because they are relatively metacommunicative. Who "it" or "she" designates depends on the context, on a double reference, first from "it" to "Wyoming" then from "Wyoming" to the concept or image of Wyoming.

*I, you,* and *it* are the algebraic $x$, $y$, and $z$ of ordinary language. They serve exactly the same purpose in speech that "unknowns" serve in math—to act as a variable function in a system so that a particular value may be assigned to each, relative to values assigned other functions in the system. For example, of three people talking together about each other any one may be *I, you,* or *it* from one moment to the next, depending on who is sender, receiver, and referent of the talk at that moment. Tom, Dick, and Harry are like numbers or particular values that may be plugged into $x$, $y$, and $z$ (*I, you* and *it*) such that if two are known, the other is known. In other words, pronouns are to proper and common nouns what algebra is to arithmetic, a further abstraction. This is why children learn how to use pronouns last.

Whereas nouns, verbs, adjectives, and some adverbs tend to name concepts of *things,* articles, prepositions, conjunctions, and some adverbs tend to name concepts of *relations.*

Adjectives name the traits by which class concepts are formed. Let's replace "articles" with the more modern grammatical notion of "determiners," which includes not only *a, an,* and *the* but *some, any, all, a few,* and any other expressions of quantity, including numbers themselves. Whereas adjectives express quality, determiners express quantity. Concepts of quantity overlap with concepts of logical relations, for *the, any, all,* and *some* also say how broadly a statement is to apply. So determiners are harder than nouns, verbs, and adjectives, quantity being generally more abstract than quality and more directly tied to logical relations.

Prepositions and conjunctions express only concepts of relations—spatial (*in, above, through*), temporal (*after, during, until*), and logical (*if, unless, because, despite*). In this way, they are fairly specialized, like determiners. Relations of time, space, and logic may also be expressed by adverbs (*now, later, farther, downward, therefore, nevertheless*). So the so-called functor words—determiners, prepositions, and conjunctions—may as a class be assumed to belong to a later stage of growth than the other parts of speech, as samples of small children's speech show. Older learners will have "acquired" all the parts of speech but will vary according to how often they use the more relational and metacommunicative words, that is, how explicitly they can *name* the connections among their concepts as opposed to egocentrically assuming them when explicitness is intended and desirable.

Reading the lists from left to right, we can summarize the increasing abstractive difficulty of parts of speech as follows:

| proper nouns | common nouns | pronouns | |
|---|---|---|---|
| | verbs | prepositions | conjunctions |
| | adjectives | determiners | adverbs of relations |
| | time-space adverbs | | |

**Growth Sequence 10: From the use of words naming *things* to words naming *time-space relations*, then to words naming *logical relations*, when explicitness is intended and desirable.**

## *Grammatical options in naming*

Parts of speech differ only secondarily in the kind of concepts they refer to; they differ first of all in the specialized grammatical role each plays in a sentence. It is not the case that nouns name only things, verbs only actions, and adjectives only qualities. The noun *descent* refers to an action, the verb *encase* to an object (casing), and the adjective *lumpy* refers to objects. In keeping with the truth that thought may be cast into alternative language forms, we could say that the pudding is lumpy or that lumps float in the pudding, depending on the desired emphasis and effect. So a certain kind of concept may take one of several parts of speech when translated into language. This is why it is misleading to define *nouns* for students only as names of a person, place, or thing, and *verbs* only as actions. All parts of speech name, and they name concepts, and several may name the same concept. The difference between the adjective *helpless* and the adverb *helplessly* is not a difference in concept but in *how one wants to get the concept into the sentence.*

To some extent, the language form into which speakers cast a concept merely reflects their choices about how to cast a more complex idea of which the concept is only a part. That is, one has options about how to get the concept of encasing or of helplessness into a statement of a larger idea. One may choose to place the concept in a subject or object role (noun) or into a modifying role (adjective or adverb), or to predicate a statement by means of it (verb). One may choose to convey causality by saying that such and such was the *cause* (noun) of the effect, that such and such *caused* the effect (verb), that the effect happened *because* such and such (conjunction), or that the effect happened *because of* such and such (preposition). The grammatical specializations of vocabulary that we call parts of speech exist to offer options about how to relate a concept to fellow concepts interacting in the same statement. Thus it is that naming depends in turn on the more inclusive process of stating.

**Growth Sequence 11: Toward increasing ability to name a concept by a part of speech befitting the role of that concept within a statement.**

## *Rhetorical options in naming*

Something may be named by more than one word. Diction, in the sense of word choice, concerns alternative naming. This goes beyond mere synonyms, which are different words for the same concept (*imitate, emulate*). You may point to your car and call it a vehicle, a sedan, a chariot, a lemon, a liability, or a relic. In your discourse these all refer to the same thing—what you are pointing to. The physical referent of all is the same, but each word applies a different conceptualization to it. So besides a choice among synonyms for the same concept, a sender has choices about how to verbally ticket nonverbal things, with the result that the receiver is influenced to regard the nonverbal item from only one of many possible viewpoints. The idea that a rose by any other name may not smell so sweet reminds us that naming guides response.

Maturity in naming relates of course to increasing size of vocabulary, but much more is required—some detachment from language and some liberation of mind, some wit. Beginners tend to fuse word with thing and only gradually differentiate symbol from symbolized to the point where they can detach a word they have associated with a thing and replace it by another name. Studying foreign languages certainly enhances this detachment, precisely by forcing the mind to accept alternative names for the same concepts. Seeing clearly the independence of matter from mind is a prerequisite for virtuosity in naming, and this is a factor of general egocentricity, because such detachment is tantamount to separating self from world (*I* from *it*).

*Figurative names*    Naming may be literal or figurative. Calling policemen *centurions* overlays on the concept of modern policemen the concept of Roman military officers and thus makes a double reference. Such metaphorical naming opens up limitless possibilities for wit and imagination, since virtually any two items in the universe may be classed alike by some attribute or other. In this way *naming can be a way of stating.* Calling policemen centurions states, in effect, that they have the professional dedication, self-discipline, and inherited esprit de corps that characterized these Roman officers. Naming figuratively is an *implicit* way of stating. In fact, the more any name departs from the most commonly used label for something, the more it tends to make an implicit statement while, or under the guise of, merely naming.

Distinguish this deliberate originality, however, from the naïve speaker's use of a single word to make a statement, exemplified in the extreme by small children's tendency to say, "Hat," for example, when they mean, "I see a hat lying over there." This way of making a word do duty as a sentence is very different of course. In both cases, a word is not only naming a concept but is relating that concept to one or more other concepts. Adults too might say, "A sail!" meaning, "I see a ship," in which case they are using the figure of speech called synecdoche (letting a part stand for a whole). The difference lies in awareness, or lack of egocentricity. In a sense, children are merely

using synecdoche too, but they have no choice, and unless the
receiver is especially close to the speaker both in the moment and
physically in general, he will not understand, because no public
convention supplies the missing elaboration.

**Growth Sequence 12: Toward increasing versatility and originality
in naming.**

# Phrasing

A phrase may name also. Some phrases name, whereas some relate concepts in ways akin to stating. So phrasing overlaps the functions of naming and stating, by expanding the first and compressing the second. A phrase is a word cluster relating the concepts that the individual words stand for. The result is a conceptual complex. Phrases add to naming the very important language operation of modifying. *Man in the moon, gesture of contempt, separate peace, delightful old coot, behind the curtain, during the war* are words brought to bear on each other so that the meaning of one is modified by the meaning of the other. This joining of concepts may create an original notion or may be so standard (*man in the moon*) as to have the force of a single concept and single word only.

Phrases modify either a noun or a verb and hence function in a sentence as an adjective or an adverb. This means they express both concepts of things and concepts of relations. Prepositional phrases treat relations directly because prepositions name relations (*near, during*). Phrasing increases enormously the variety of ways things can be named. The lexicon of a language is finite, but the permutations of this lexicon by phrasing are virtually infinite.

Suppose a speaker does not know the name for a public concept. It she doesn't know the word *nave,* she will have to resort to talking around the concept—to a circumlocution—such as "the part of the church running lengthwise." In this case, phrasing indicates lack of growth in vocabulary. Often youngsters' concepts outstrip their vocabulary and force them to invent. Phrasing of this sort shows clearly the disparity in growth between thought and speech and also shows how the presence or absence of a certain word is no accurate index to the presence or absence of certain concepts.

Phrasing from necessity spurs invention, however, and some of it has the virtue of originality. A fourth grader writing about his trip to New York City referred to the Statue of Liberty as "that big metal girl," having forgotten the name. Fresh phrasing like this re-creates the world. It can amuse us, make us see old things in a new way, and understate. The power of poetry depends tremendously on originality of phrasing, to name anew and relate the normally unrelated.

In a kind of parody of their future growth, the fourth grader's phrase and preschooler's "Hat" do out of necessity and naivete what the best users of language do. Once again, the surface form of the language does not show this difference. Growth of phrasing consists of doing with foreknowledge of effect what the fourth grader did as makeshift. In the play *Cyrano de Bergerac,* Cyrano reels off a fanciful catalogue of the ways in which his detractor might have referred to

Cyrano's nose had he the wit to make his insults imaginative. Though not executed in phrases only, his tour de force exemplifies the high art of versatile and original referring that extends beyond the word and that learners grow toward. Skilled language-users don't always *want* to use the conventional term for a concept, because they can get various rhetorical effects by a creative circumlocution.

Furthermore, words do not exist for everything that can be conceived. Any trait whatsoever, visible or invisible, can be the defining characteristic of a class. Concept formation can be very personal. People classify other people, for example, into those who are safe or dangerous, useful or useless, attractive or repulsive, stable or flighty, and so on. Anyone can form a class concept any time merely by designating the trait or traits that would identify instances of the collection, just as anyone could decide to form a club whose members would all be left-handed Bach-loving expatriates. The more original the thinking, the more original will have to be the naming and phrasing of it. Vocabulary alone tends to stereotype thought. The only way to offset this is to combine vocabulary in unusual ways by making up phrases.

**Growth Sequence 13: Metaphor and circumlocution enter more and more into the learner's language as a way not to substitute for lack of vocabulary but to express a greater range of thought in a greater range of styles for a greater range of effects.**

By bringing parts of speech to bear on each other, phrases explicitly relate one concept to another and hence approach the role of stating. Many a clause could in fact be a phrase (". . . after the show was over . . ." or ". . . at the end of the show . . ."). Reduced clauses or potential clauses will be treated below as statement, but it's important to keep in mind that an option nearly always exists to relate concepts as a phrase or as a clause. One chooses whether to assert the relation as a statement, thereby giving it more importance, or to subordinate the relation within a statement asserting something else.

# Stating

Stating is saying something is so. Like a phrase, a statement relates concepts, but a statement does more. It *predicates.* By means of a predicate, the speaker asserts a proposition. So verbs are the key, and the nature of the predicate determines the kind of statement. Grammatically, a statement corresponds to a clause, not to a sentence necessarily, since a sentence may contain many clauses. The independent clause corresponds in language to a proposition in logic. It is the fundamental arena of grammar, which is the sum of ways that words and phrases may be related to make statements.

The first issue of growth in stating is whether speakers can parcel their thought out into at least a subject and a predicate and perhaps some modifiers of each. If they make a statement through a single word or through a phrase, they are obviously leaving out elements and therefore making their statement implicitly. As we said, immature speakers let a part stand egocentrically for the whole they have in mind—by default—whereas poets compress thought into figures of speech that—by design—imply whole statements.

## *Modification*

Once capable of stating in clauses, learners face a second and very long-range issue of whether their clauses explicitly elaborate in language forms—to the extent they think they do and to the extent their receiver needs—just what they have in mind. Consider language as a kind of adjustable rack to fit thought onto. The more people spell out just what they mean, the more they do what we earlier called elaborating. The way to make ideas explicit is to put into words enough details about the subject and the predicate to connect up with shared assumptions in the receiver. This means adding modifiers— qualification, quantification, time, place, manner. This is the function of determiners, adjectives, and adverbs—whether in the form of a word or a word cluster.

The amount of modification is the key to innumerable composition and comprehension matters. Overgeneralizing, for example, results from failing to quantify (to say how many people or things are covered by one's statement) or to qualify (to limit the subject or object by more detailed description and limit the conditions under which the statement is true). Both narrative and generalization may suffer if the time and space are indicated too vaguely. Paucity of vivifying detail and unclear concepts require more, or more precise, modification. Above all, the predicate itself must become as complex as the thought is complex. For example, compare these two sentences:

The middle child in the family has the best deal.

A middle child may enjoy the advantages of having the elder fray a path for her and shoulder the most responsibility and yet not be treated as the baby of the family.

The first statement may imply the second, but does the receiver know that? At the grammatical level, explicitness entails more words and more interaction of words—verbal complexity.

**Growth Sequence 14: Toward increasing modification as required by the complexity of ideas and the needs of the receiver.**

## The Special case of to be

The verb *to be* requires special attention. It means several different things logically and hence tends to be widely used and ambiguous. It is the most important predicate. The notation of symbolic logic differentiates the various logical meanings of *to be,* by assigning to each its own symbol. For the best explanation of this important problem of translating thought into speech, we quote from logician Suzanne Langer:

Few people are aware that they use so common and important a word as *is* in half a dozen different senses. Consider, for instance the following propositions:

**1.** The rose is red.

**2.** Rome is greater than Athens.

**3.** Barbarossa is Frederick I.

**4.** Barbarossa is a legendary hero.

**5.** To sleep is to dream.

**6.** God is.

In each of these sentences we find the verb "is." But each sentence expresses a differently constructed proposition: (1) ascribes a *property* to a term; in (2) "is" has logically only an auxiliary value of *asserting* the dyadic relation, "greater than"; in (3) "is" expresses *identity;* in (4) "is" indicates *membership* in a class (the class of legendary heroes); (5) "is" means *entailment* (sleeping entails dreaming); in (6) "is" equals *existence.*

So we see that in (1) and (2) it is only part of the logical verb—it serves only to assert the relation, which is otherwise expressed—and in the remaining four cases, where "is" does function as the whole logical verb, it expresses a different relation in every case. It has at least four different meanings besides its use as auxiliary. Our linguistic means of conveying relations are highly ambiguous. But the expression of relations is the chief purpose of language. If we were interested only in *things* and not in their arrangement and connection, we could express ourselves with our forefingers. . . . the study of relations is necessarily bound up with a study of discourse. But if the latter obscures and disguises relations, as it often does, there is no escape from error, except by adopting another sort of discourse altogether. Such a new medium of expression is the symbolism of logic. In this ideography, the four propositions wherein "is" really names a relation would not appear to have a common form, but would wear the badge of their distinctions plainly in view:

3. Barbarossa = Frederick I

4. Barbarossa ∈ legendary hero

5. To sleep ⊂ to dream

6. E! God*

**Growth Sequence 15: Toward increasing ability to differentiate, as sender and receiver, the various meanings of *to be*.**

## *Tense as abstraction level*

If modifying *elaborates* statements, what *generalizes* them? The answer is, the tense of the verb that predicates the statement. What people generally call time differences are really degrees of abstraction. Distances between sender, receiver, and message amount to differences in levels of abstraction.** Tenses describe when events occurred in relation to when the speaker is referring to them. Hence they denote point of view or the distance between the speaker and the original raw material that she has abstracted from. Besides, it is clear that people predicate about a lot besides events and that time is not an issue except in narrative.

One way learners grow in the skill of stating is to assert explicitly more general statements. They may learn how to form all the tenses fairly early, but they will actually compose and comprehend state-

* Susanne Langer, *Introduction to Symbolic Logic*, Dover Publications, Inc., New York, 1953. pp. 56-57. Reprinted by permission of the publisher
**For development of this idea see *Teaching the Universe of Discourse*, 1983. James Moffett (Boynton/Cook, Portsmouth, NH).

ments in certain ones only as they grow into the abstraction levels the tenses exist to convey.

The present tense of generalization predicates explicitly, as its name says, the analogizing of experiences of different times. It is an utterly different tense from the present progressive. *What happens* can only be recurring—that is, mental—events. "He eats catsup on his scrambled eggs" expresses a higher generalization than "He is eating catsup on his eggs," "He was eating catsup on his eggs," "He ate catsup on his eggs," or "He will eat catsup on his eggs." "He *eats* catsup on his eggs" *summarizes* all the other statements. Each statement in order summarizes, in fact, a bit more than the preceding one. Each tense applies more broadly over time and space until the sequence culminates in that tense that specializes in stating generalities as such.

**Growth Sequence 16: Toward increasingly general statement as indicated by the tense sequence below:**

| *what is happening*—progressive present |
| --- |

*what has happened*—perfect

| *what happened*—past |
| --- |

*what will happen*—future

| *what happens*—present tense of generalization |
| --- |

*what might or could happen or be true*—conditional

The boxed tenses here show most clearly the main expansion from present to past to timeless, the other tenses fitting between these. Further generalizing the past leads to *what will happen.* The future is only an extrapolation of the past. Extrapolation is a mental extension over time and space of existing circumstances. Convinced by their analogies between past events that life has stability and consistency, learners predict that certain objects will reappear or events recur. But *nothing* ever recurs, of course. Establishing parallels between *what has happened* and *what will happen* is a matter of generalizing experience further: "The sun has always risen, and the sun will continue to rise." The next logical step is to generalize that "The sun always rises."

The shift from past to potential truth is a shift from fact in the Latin sense of *factus*—the "done," the deed or event—toward opinion. The growth sequence is that people record experience via perception, then report it via memory, then generalize it via reflection. Not only are these stages by which anyone processes experience all the time, they are stages of growth accumulated by all youngsters. As perception, memory, and reason successively develop, youngsters make and understand increasingly more statements in the corresponding tense.

**Growth Sequence 17: From emphasis on the present (sensorimotor abstracting) to past (memory abstracting) to timelessness (abstracting by reason).**

If we look at the conditional tenses, we can see that further reasoning will take us beyond statement to the *relations among* statements. "If this happens, that will happen" (or will have happened). "If this happened, that would happen." "If this had happened, that would have happened." These tenses are coordinated as a function of each other. The reasoning resides not in one tense but in the relation of tenses. The truth of one statement is conditional on the other statement being true. The conditional tense breaks the bounds of the clause and forces us to consider how statements are connected to each other.

# Chaining

The clause, not the sentence, is the basic verbal form of statement. When teachers define a sentence as subject plus predicate, they are really defining a clause, and when they say a sentence expresses a complete thought, they mean an independent clause asserts a proposition. They are thinking of a single clause as a sentence, whereas a sentence may comprise several clauses. Indeed, a sentence is the main way clauses are chained.

## Sentences

A set of clause-statements may be connected in three ways:

1. By making each a separate sentence and stringing them:
   *I saw Bobby's hat. It was in a tree. The wind blew it there. Then it rained.*

2. By joining several into one sentence by conjunctions, relative pronouns, or punctuation:
   *I saw Bobby's hat and it was in a tree, and the wind blew it there, and then it rained.* (The famous run-on sentence of the immature speaker.)
   *I saw Bobby's hat, which was in a tree, where the wind blew it before it rained.*

3. By reducing some clauses to phrases and embedding them in others:
   *In a tree I saw Bobby's hat, blown there by the wind before the rain came.*

First, learners predicate ideas separately; then they join them with the easier conjunctions; then sometimes they join them with more difficult conjunctions and relative pronouns, and sometimes they embed some within others. So 1, 2, and 3 above represent a growth order if you keep in mind that the difficulty of conjoining (2) depends on the difficulty of the connector word (its concept, that is), and that the difficulty of embedding (3) varies considerably with the kind of clause reduction.

To demonstrate further the issue of 2 and 3, let's take another series having a more abstract topic:

1. Goodsayer was elected. He adopted the policies advocated by his opponent. He had harshly criticized them when he was running for office.

Notice the repetition of subject and object so clangingly present in children's clause strings but muted here by the pronouns. Strings are

47

uneconomical because they keep predicating the same nominals. Personal pronouns disguise this, but of pronouns only the relative can solve this, not the personal (*he* above). The next sentence represents maturer development by conjoining the clauses:

2. After he was elected, Goodsayer adopted the policies that his opponent was advocating, which he had harshly criticized when he was running for office.

But the following version, which reduces and embeds four clauses from the first, requires substantially more development:

3. Once elected, Goodsayer adopted the policies advocated by his opponent—the very policies he had harshly criticized during the campaign.

It is worth the trouble to study these three sentences and compare the changes, because the differences exemplify a great deal about growth in sentence development. Though shorter, the last sentence is harder than the second because students have to develop clauses first before they can learn to reduce them. Of course, a speaker or writer does not normally compare alternatives, as we are doing here. Most composition is more spontaneous than that, and even hard revision would not produce the shorter version until the author had logged considerable composing experience. Compactness comes harder, and when length is a sign of looseness, as in run-on sentences, it shows immaturity.

This is not to say the compacter version is always better. It has a different emphasis, partly because it leaves more implicit. It might not therefore suit as well a given intent. The point here is that to be *able* to reduce clauses and embed them in each other, when this relates concepts appropriately, indicates fairly advanced growth. Of course, "reducing and embedding clauses" is only a manner of speaking since no one sees people do this except occasionally perhaps in written revision, but to infer some such inner process gradually occurring seems reasonable since language users of different maturity levels differ by just such sample sentences. Inserting links between clauses is easier than reducing and fusing clauses, but the conceptual difficulty of individual linking words—spatial-temporal versus logical conjunctions, for example—must be allowed for.

As clauses are conjoined and embedded, they require certain meta-communicative words—conjunctions like *but, or, although, because, unless* or relative pronouns like *who, which,* and *where.* The statements are the communication, and these connectors metacommunicate about how to take and relate the statements. As we said, such words are harder just as concepts, but they are also hard because they relate statements to form more complex ideas. Conjunctions name explicitly the relation, whereas relative pronouns merely plug one nominal into two predicates, naming nothing and relating implicitly instead. See preceding examples.

**Growth Sequence 18: Expanding the repertory of clause-connecting options as follows:**

- **String of separate independent clauses, each a sentence**
- **Clauses conjoined by coordinating conjunctions (*and, but, or*) and time-space conjunctions**
- **Clauses conjoined by logical subordinating conjunctions and fused by relative pronouns**
- **Clauses reduced and embedded in each other**

Two things are important to the formulation above. One is to emphasize that mature learners not only can do these things but do them *appropriately,* according to the place of the statements in a total discourse. Complexity for its own sake is no mark of maturity. Complexity is necessary but not sufficient for fullest growth. A string of single-clause sentences can be very effective for making an image or idea dawn gradually on the receiver. It understates and it also stretches out the reader's assimilation time. Mature students would for these reasons employ such a string even though they were capable of fashioning very intricate sentence structures.

The second matter is the critical one of subordinating concepts one to another so that they are related with the proper emphasis. Stringing makes all statements equal, besides not making explicit the relations among them. The only connection is the primitive one of first-to-last, which says nothing unless the statements are about events, in which case the order of stringing is assumed to be the order of their occurrence. Coordinating conjunctions say that the statements are equal in rank (*co*-ordinate) in addition to being, say alternative (or) or adversative (but). More properly speaking, the statements are equal and the conjunctions are coordinating because equality is in the nature of the logical relationships *and, or,* and *but,* if you think about it, whereas the subordinating conjunctions, such as proviso (unless), concessions (*although*), condition (*if*), and the time-space conjunctions require that the clause they introduce be subordinate to the one to which it is conjoined. (Time-space clauses

are always adverbial modifiers of course, and hence subordinated to
the sentence predicate.)

Now let's bring in the conventional terms:

- Single-clause sentence—"simple sentence"
- Clauses conjoined by coordinating conjunctions—"compound sentence"
- Clauses conjoined by subordinating conjunctions—"complex sentence"
- Clauses conjoined by both coordinating and subordinating conjunctions—"compound-complex sentence"

Although this progression roughly parallels our growth sequence, it
allows neither for the embedding of reduced clauses nor for the
variation in the difficulty among conjunctions and between conjunctions and relative pronouns. This old classification of sentences does
bring out, however, subordination and emphasis, two critical factors
of growth in making sentences and sentence sequences out of basic
statements.

From his research with children's writing Kellogg Hunt concluded that sentence growth is marked by (1) increasing modification
of nouns by large clusters of adjectives, relative clauses, and reduced
relative clauses; (2) increasing use of nominalizations other than
nouns and pronouns for subjects and objects (clauses, infinitival and
gerundive constructions), and (3) embedding of sentences to an increasing depth (entailed by 1 and 2).* A sentence having a single
word or phrase for a subject ("*Such an idea* never occurred to her.")
is easier to formulate than one having a clause for a subject ("*What
other people might think of her actions* doesn't concern her."). In the
second example, the nominalization, in italics, is a clause embedded
in the clause of the whole sentence and containing, as its own
subject, a nominal phrase ("other people") like that serving in the
first example as subject of the whole sentence ("Such an idea").

**Growth Sequence 19: Toward increasing versatility in constructing
sentences, exploiting more nearly the total resources inherent in
*modifying*, *conjoining*, *reducing*, and *embedding* clauses; and
toward increasing comprehension of sentences of such range.**

---

* Kellogg Hunt, *Grammatical Structures Written at Three Grade Levels*, National
Council of Teachers of English, Champaign, IL, 1965

## Syllogisms

A special case of conjoining clauses was touched on when we spoke of conditional tenses joined by *if.* When two or more conditional clauses are linked to each other and to a conclusion clause, a syllogism is created. "If high spending contributes to inflation, and if advertising and credit stimulate high spending, then advertising and credit contribute to inflation."

At the material level, such a conjunction of conditions may be stated in a sentence like this: "*If* heavy rain falls a long time on loose dirt, and *if* the terrain is steeply tilted, a mudslide will occur." Note that this logical relationship may be expressed by other conjunctions and by adverbs: "A mudslide occurs *because* heavy rain falls a long time on loose dirt and *because* the terrain is steeply tilted." Or: "The rain falls a long time on loose dirt, and the terrain is steeply tilted; so [*therefore*] a mudslide occurs." The point is that underneath these various conjunctions and adverbs there lies a single logical relationship. This relationship is called entailment—certain things being so entail other things being so. (See on page 43 Susanne Langer's mention of entailment.) It is important to realize that what is the same at the conceptual level—entailment—may be expressed at the verbal level as causality, conditionality, or something else.

Syllogizing may be, first of all, implicit or explicit and, second, may take several forms. It is an important sort of logical growth to look for, but the teacher can expect it to be revealed in more than one verbal way, if made explicit at all. A syllogism may perfectly well exist in a discourse without being verbalized in a single sentence. It may be embodied in another kind of linguistic linking than conjoined clauses—in one of the other kinds of chaining discussed next.

## Transitional words

Besides conjunctions and relative pronouns, certain adverbs connect clauses and do so explicitly as conjunctions (*moreover, however, nevertheless, so, therefore, accordingly,* and others referring to ideas in previous clauses), but these differ in being situated *within* a clause, not between clauses, so that they tie clauses together only by throwing an idea bridge, not by connecting grammatically. These are what we might call transition words, because they are added to a clause to relate statements explicitly in the same way that whole sentences may be stuck into a discourse to effect transitions from one main idea or part of the organization to another ("Leaving aside for the moment the objections to this idea, let's now turn to . . . .").

Transitions, too, constitute meta-communication and hence do not occur to speakers or writers too egocentric to realize that an audience might not know how to connect their clauses unless guided. On the other hand, mature communicators may choose to omit some transitions as being unnecessary, heavy, or verbose for the ideas and the audience involved, or may wish to speak implicitly to make their audience think more and work out connections for itself—obviously a sophisticated stance, indeed a very confident one. And once again, the presence of the words—*hence* or *so,* say—does not guarantee the presence of the concepts they stand for. A trick of weak writers is to plaster their composition together with *therefores* and *moreovers* in *lieu* of thought.

## *Punctuation*

Colons, semicolons, and sometimes commas also connect statements. They are much less explicit than word connectors, but they have some meaning. A colon tends to act as an equation mark and hence assumes one meaning of *to be* (identity), and a semicolon or comma implies unusual closeness between clause-statements. Without indicating the nature of the relation, this binding nevertheless invites readers to supply for themselves a conjunction of time, causality, contradiction, and so on, according to context.

## *Paragraphing*

Paragraphing is another way of implying relations between statements. A paragraph break, for example, between one statement and another means that the thought takes a bigger jump than is usual between sentences or that thought is shifting to another time or plane or domain. Placing one statement at the beginning of a paragraph and another within may mean that the first is superordinate or more general and that the next one is subordinate or more concrete. The first sentence might state a generality and the second state an instance or consequence of it. The relative positioning may obviate the need of "for example" or "so." The sheer order in which statements are chained means something of course, since juggling the order would usually make considerable difference in the intelligibility of the message. Paragraphing imposes upon this sequence other patterns of significance by clumping together statements so that distance, salience, and subordination vary among them and hence imply certain interrelations. The ways of chaining sentences that comprise paragraphs can comprise the organization of an entire discourse.

## *Organization*

The possibilities of paragraphing are the possibilities of organizing a whole discourse. The continuity may vary in length, but once beyond the sentence (with its special grammatical rules of relating) the ways of chaining statements are the same as for composing the units of any other linear medium—serial order, juxtaposition, and pattern. These are universal factors of form and constitute what English teachers mean by "organization" in a composition. Form establishes relations by sheer selection and arrangement, without naming relations. Form speaks—but implicitly. So clause-connecting throughout an entire continuity of statements is nothing less than the overall form of a complete discourse, and the forms with which people compose discourses are general forms common to many other media.

*Ascending and descending forms*    In music, we speak of the first statement of a theme and of its later variations. This form compares to an opening statement of the main idea of a discourse followed by the elaborating of its implication in substatements. Either a whole discourse, a subdivision of it, a paragraph, or even a sentence could be organized this way—from higher to lower abstraction. It is the deductive form exemplified by the famous "topic sentence," which sets a frame within which details, implications, consequences, evidence, and so on are then expounded. Within a sentence this works out as a main clause followed by subordinate clauses and by modifiers:

> They just had to peer over the rim, although the canyon terrified
> them, leaning far forward over planted feet, heads tipped back for
> balance, eyes turned down their cheeks.

Within a whole discourse, paragraphs would so descend.

The opposite form may be equally right, depending on intent and content. It is the inductive order, by which a theme is gradually built up through partial statements until arrived at climactically. Within a sentence, modifiers and subordinate clauses would prepare for the main clause, which would come at the end as climax (the so-called periodic sentence).

> Whenever someone asked her to sing once again, perhaps at tea time
> in the old sunroom, perhaps at a garden gathering in the morning,
> imploring, saying she had no right to withhold that gift, her plump
> hand would go to her throat, and her head would slowly wag no.

Following the same model on larger scales, a paragraph or a whole discourse would start low and build high, suspensefully, revealing only enough per statement to carry the receiver to the next, broader view, whether the increments are physical details of a complex object, causes of some effect, or arguments leading toward a conclusion. *Various orders*    The direction that the chaining moves between low and high abstraction, whole and part, generality and instance, is of great significance for composition and comprehension, for the opposed approaches orient the receiver very differently. The growing learner has to understand that these options exist and what effects they have. Chaining need not follow the order in which events, images, or thoughts originally or logically occur, because rhetorical ends must be served. A reader may see a scene more clearly if the writer starts with a panoramic shot and then zooms in on details, but like William Faulkner and Stephen Crane on occasion, the writer may want the reader to experience with the character the feeling, precisely, of *not* being on top of a situation. An effect of dawning, produced in many poems, comes from forcing the receivers to orient themselves by minimal cues that imply perhaps several possibilities that must be considered and checked out as the statement continuity proceeds. A logical conclusion might go either at the beginning or at the end of a discourse, depending on whether the reader's knowing the conclusion first makes following the arguments much easier or on whether the writer wishes readers to work through in their own minds the steps by which the conclusion was reached.

It may be better to derange the order in which events occurred and start in the middle, as Homer did with the *Iliad,* then flash back to the beginning, or to cut back and forth among different periods, as Marcel Proust and Kurt Vonnegut do, in order to juxtapose events in a new, mental relation. Inductive and deductive orders may be combined as when a main statement is built up by evidence then, once established and warranted, applied to various domains to see what it will turn up. Repetition is also an important formal device common to both writing and music as the "motif."

**Growth Sequence 20: Toward using and responding to the full rhetorical possibilities for chaining statements by grammar, transitional words, punctuation, paragraphing, and organizational form, according to the commitment of the whole discourse.**

Emphasis must be on good judgment in playing options. No particular sentence construction, paragraph structure, or organizational form is better than another except relative to the communication needs of the content and intent. Growth does not consist of merely acquiring the tools of metacommunication to name or state connections explicitly. These tools constitute the technical prerequisite but alone are not enough. Always, the learner must learn to judge, as either sender or receiver, if metacommunication is desirable. Too often teachers incline to value only the explicit, because they can see it and thereby *know* what a student's thought is, but explicitness is definitely only half of the matter. Since not all can ever be said, discoursing is always a matter of ascertaining how much will do the trick properly.

A concept may play different roles in a complex of concepts, may be more or less conscious in the speaker, may be more or less explicit in a discourse, and so may for these reasons be conveyed by a single word, a phrase, a simple sentence, a complex sentence, a continuity of sentences, a metaphor, a motif, or a formal pattern in the organization of the total work. A learner grows in mastery of composing and comprehending these alternatives for matching thought with speech.

# Growth in Kinds of Discourse

Discourse begins in dialogue. Children first learn to speak from conversing. Dialogue is verbal collaboration, which means that utterances are chained by the reciprocal prompting of each speaker by the other. Sender and receiver constantly reverse roles. Feedback and correction are plentiful and fast. Statements are mixed with questions, because speakers can get immediate answers, and mixed with commands, because speakers are localized together in the same space-time and hence more personally related. The *I-you* relation dominates the discourse, in fact, so that the organization is determined by a succession of social exchanges even when the dialogue is an earnest intellectual discussion sticking close to a topic. Dialogue may of course vary tremendously in maturity but the less developed a speaker the more she is *limited* to dialogue. *Growth consists of extending one's range of kinds of discourse by learning to monologue at different abstraction levels.*

Monologue arises from dialogue. One speaker solos for a while within the context of a conversation to tell an anecdote, describe something she saw, explain a point of view, give a set of directions, or otherwise *sustain some continuity.* Thus are narrative, exposition, and argumentation born. Most kinds of discourse are monologue and, in self-contained form, are written. To compose and to comprehend most discourse, then, the learner must learn to spin out from within herself some monological continuities based on the kinds of logical and rhetorical chaining that we have described. She must forego at times the give-and-take prompting and fast feedback of dialogical succession.

It takes emotional as well as conceptual and verbal maturity to compose alone, even just orally (though once able, a person may verbalize compulsively as a defense!). To shift from collaborating to soloing is only one case of the general law that external activity becomes internalized. As mind digests matter, so personality incorporates sociality. Furthermore, composing monologues requires a certain inner attention to the ordering of thoughts and an understanding of the receiver's need for some elaboration. Comprehending monologues requires an ability to focus steadily on one thing and to hold in the mind a stream of accumulating statements until they can be assimilated.

**Growth Sequence 21: From mixing various kinds of discourse within dialogue to singling out and sustaining each kind of discourse separately in monologue.**

At first, children talk indiscriminately to themselves and to their toys and to their partners at play. Even if you teach senior high students, it is important to understand this play prattle, because it is a base line from which all later growth can be better perceived. The first monologuing is very egocentric in that it does not allow much at all for an audience other than the speaker. (Adults accuse each other of talking only to themselves when they feel discourse is not "objective" enough.) Also, the subject is something present in front of the child—something she is watching or playing with. Actually, the subject is the child's feelings about what is present. Invoking our communication triad (page 58), prattle represents speaker, listener, and subject at a point where egocentricity makes them barely separate. A lot of prattle does not, in fact, even attempt to communicate but represents sheer vocal exercise and sound games, word play.

Gradually this egocentric monologuing begins to divide into external speech aimed at other people and internal speech for oneself that goes underground and becomes merely thought as the child begins to discriminate between herself and others. Verbal thinking then goes inward and merges with nonverbal thinking. Once more socially aware, there is seldom point to "thinking out loud."

In the same way that she begins to discriminate between talking to herself and talking to others, the child begins to discriminate between talking about herself and talking about other things. From prattle focused entirely on her involvement with things facing her here and now, she turns to subjects out of sight but not out of mind and thence gradually extends for the rest of her life the space-time compass of what she discourses about. She talks about absent people and objects, events she remembers, and things to do later. This movement of growth away from self occurs over both physical and psychological distance and results in increasingly clearer separation of speaker from subject. The three-way fission of verbalization into distinct "persons," schematized in Figure 2, describes in one way the decline of egocentricity and the rise of impartiality, because another way of viewing composition and comprehension problems is as a blurring of one's mind with the world and with other minds. But true growth merely *enables* a person to achieve this analytical clarity; it does not enforce it.

## Varieties of monologue

Once launched into monologuing and the differentiation of sender, message, and receiver, the learner then begins to differentiate among the various kinds of discourse so that she can match them to her gradually diversifying thought. Prattle about play objects leads directly to labels and captions, a kind of discourse in which one says what one sees, or comments on what one sees, and which consists often of single words and sentence fragments like a child's disjointed speech. Word play clearly derives from and extends to more sophisticated levels the creative experimentation with sound and sense, the playful vocal exercising, that characterizes so much of prattle. Invented dialogue and actual dialogue are of course a direct outgrowth of child-family conversation and ultimately cover the greatest range of subject matter. Though word play, labels and captions, and actual and invented dialogue spin off directly from a child's first oral speech, they all exist also in written form, so that growth is partly a matter of carrying these kinds of discourse over into writing and reading.

Invented stories, true stories, directions, information, and ideas are first done orally as fragments of dialogue—an anecdote here, a scrap of fact here—but as whole discourses unto themselves, they are most likely done in writing. True stories take off from the here and now of prattle, other running commentary, and such sense-bound discourse as labels and captions and provide a fitting language form for memory, either that of the author or of someone she is drawing from as a source. Narrative shifts discourse up the abstraction scale, in other words, to accord on the one hand with whatever higher conceptualization memory represents over the senses, and on the other hand with whatever higher verbalization sustained monologue represents over the partnering of dialogue.

### In the literal mode

We have said that the learner expands from the present to the past to the future and then to the timeless so that the tense of her predicates is an index to her relative emphasis among sensation, memory, and

**Figure 2**
Growth of Communication Triad

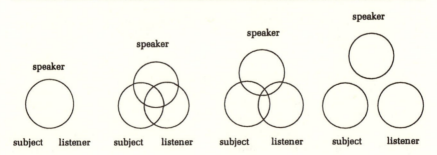

reason. It is one thing to predicate one sentence in a certain tense but quite another to make that tense predominate throughout a whole discourse. The dominant tense of a discourse establishes the abstraction level—if the discourse is in the literal mode. Preschoolers can state a generality in the present tense of generalization, but they will have to grow considerably before they *monologue*—chain a string of statements—in that tense. Actually, the predominance of a higher tense does not mean that it appears quantitatively more than another; the bulk of many an essay of generalization consists of past-tense documentation of only a few generalities, which dominate by forming the superstructure of the discourse, whereas the necessarily longer narrative elements only support.

So entire discourses may be scaled in composing and comprehending difficulty according to the abstraction level of the dominant tense. A blow-by-blow sportscast runs entirely in the present progressive (halftime generalizations are another matter!), and a traditional novel runs off almost entirely in the past tense. A highly theoretical work will consist, on the other hand, entirely of the present tense of generalization led by conditionals. Here is one way of representing lower and higher discourse continuities:

| | |
|---|---|
| now . . . now | present |
| then . . . then | past |
| if . . . then | general |

A common mixture, however, interweaves narrative documentation or illustration with timeless generality:

then . . . then . . . if . . . then


**Growth Sequence 22: Toward discourse increasingly expanded across time and space as indicated by overall organization and dominance of tense.**


### Monologues in the literal mode

| WHAT IS HAPPENING | Prattle | Recording |
|---|---|---|
| | Interior Monologue | |
| | Blow-by-blow accounts | |
| | Captions | |
| | Field and lab notes | |
| | Letters | (Point of view from |
| | Journals | within events not yet ended) |

| WHAT HAPPENED | Autobiography | Reporting |
| | Memoir | |
| | Biography | |
| | Reportage | |
| | Chronicle | |
| | History | |
| | | |
| WHAT HAPPENS | Articles of factual | Generalizing |
| | generalization | |
| | Essays of idea | |
| | generalization | |
| | | |
| WHAT COULD OR | Essays of argumen- | Theorizing |
| MAY HAPPEN | tation theory | |
| | Science, philosophy, | |
| | and mathematics | |

The order from letters and journals through chronicle and history is a whole progression within itself based on a shift from present to past and from author to other(s) as subject (first to third person, singular then plural). This is a growth order in the sense too that higher orders depend on and subsume lower ones. Generalizations about humanity, for example, may be based on history, which is based on source documents like memoirs and archives. Biography digests letters and diaries, and reportage abstracts ongoing notes. Students working at higher levels will have to draw on their own or others' work at lower levels. This absorption of lower by higher discourses corresponds to the hierarchical abstracting that takes place in the nervous system as people make information internally. Surely, being able to do this intuitively with raw material must be some kind of prerequisite for doing it consciously with discourse.

Let's examine now the following ten kinds of discourse, which are to some extent also ways of cognizing.

Word Play*

Labels and Captions

Invented Dialogue*

Actual Dialogue

Letters and Memoranda

Directions

Invented Stories*

True Stories

Information

Ideas

Leaving aside for the moment the special nature of figurative discourse (marked by asterisks), we have a crude growth progression in that dialogue comes early, letters and memoranda are dialogue-at-a-distance, and labels and captions are directly bound to sensory objects or images, whereas the last five follow the order of narrative to generalization. Directions, invented stories, and true stories are bracketed together because they follow chronological order, for the most part, and so are roughly on a par, as are information and ideas at their level of *what happens.*\*

Younger learners will find later discourse areas hard to work in, but even primary children may practice language in all ten areas concurrently, either by speaking some kinds before they can write them, or reading them before they can speak them, or by sending and receiving very short instead of long continuities. So this list indicates developmental sequence only in a very rough way: students may be expected to cover the lower areas sooner than the higher.

It is essential to understand, however, that all students will be working in all areas all the time. Although some higher areas build, in a sense, on some lower ones, it is definitely not necessary to hold off work in higher ones pending "completion" of lower ones. No one kind of discourse ever gets completed because these are lifelong learning categories. Not only is it true that less developed learners should be given credit for what they are able to comprehend and compose orally in an area of discourse, but by practicing orally they are learning the bulk of what they need to know in order to read and write in that area.

If one understands well the way in which naming, phrasing, stating, and chaining are nested within each other so that larger governs smaller, then it should be clear why it is undesirable and unnecessary to rig separate instructional sequences for vocabulary, grammar, paragraphing, and organization. Working within discourses of different abstractive levels ensures that students will come to grips with all the issues of diction, sentence construction, and organization. If students spread their work from easier to harder discourse areas in the directions we have indicated, this will of itself automatically program sequences at all language levels. Shifting, say, from narrative discourse to that of explicit generalization necessarily entails shifts in language and rhetoric and thus tends to bring successively to the fore different language structures and compositional issues.

---

\* For the theoretical development of this spectrum of discourse, see *Teaching the Universe of Discourse.* For practical application of it, see *Student-Centered Language Arts K--12,* Part III of which is organized by it.

Tense, as indicated, is one thing that changes. But so do other things. Adverbial phrases and clauses of time, place, and manner that abound in recording and reporting give way, in generalization and theory, to phrases and clauses of qualification; temporal connectives, transitions, and organization perforce yield to logical ones. The kinds of paragraph structure one uses tend to shift. Labeling and captioning naturally focus on names, phrases, and single sentences. Things named in fables *must* be figurative. If teachers counsel their students well about which sort of discourse to tackle next, they will also be sequencing work in the substructures of discourse. The detail with which we have treated naming, phrasing, stating, and chaining aims to show how one can detect growth in these substructures, not how to sequence them in isolation. Assessing growth of substructures is one way of helping teachers evaluate and recommend whole discourses.

**Growth Sequence 23: Toward a more fully discriminated and articulated repertory of kinds of discourse in which to practice composing and comprehending.**

## In the figurative mode

Invented dialogue and invented stories cover plays and fiction, of course, in which characters, settings, and actions are themselves figures of speech, standing, as they do, for aspects of experience. Word play covers the juggling of meaning for its own sake, but figurative language occurs obviously in any kind of discourse. It's just that in word play it may be the whole discourse, as in a pun.

Poetry, plays, and fiction are not just what they seem. On the surface, script and transcript, novel and biography look exactly alike, and judging from the language forms only, we would often not be able to tell real from invented. The difference is the other dimension or so of meaning given these works by the kind of ricocheting of reference among items inside and outside the text that we discussed as the figurative use of language. Taken literally, factually, a poem, novel, or play seems to represent no higher skill to read or write than the prattle, true story, or actual dialogue that each respectively simulates. But of course in simulating rather than factually abstracting, an author is in fact abstracting at a much higher level than the form he simulates. *In telling what happened, a novelist is also telling what happens.* The difference between *King Lear* and a transcript of a local hearing, which as written dialogue it resembles, lies in the nature of artful, multileveled composition.

Author's of imaginative literature are not just *abstracting* directly up from the ground in the manner described for abstracting from. To some extent they are composing, over that sort of abstracting, another sort. Their people, places, actions, and objects are already themselves abstractions of others they stand for. Putting these into play creates a much higher abstraction, in fact, than merely reporting or dramatizing what some real people actually did, unless, as with case histories, the real personages and actions have been especially chosen because they will be taken figuratively as tokens of a type. The more meaningful in this way is a case history or biography the more it must be selectively composed like a play or novel. Art is a double editing of reality, once by the holistic mode and once by the linear, and selectivity is the key to making a literary work operate both literally and figuratively at once.

Put it this way. Characters in literature, including children's literature, are concepts. The Wizard of Oz, the Three Billy Goats Gruff with Troll, Alice and the Red Queen and White Knight are concepts. So are Hamlet, Oedipus, and the Man with the Gray Flannel Suit. So too are the settings and the key physical objects of literature—the church tower in *The Master Builder,* the ring in the Tolkien trilogy, West Egg in *The Great Gatsby,* the way stations in *Heart of Darkness,* and the moldering wedding cake in *Great Expectations.* These concepts are not explicitly stated and can be grasped only by means of everything else in the work. The ultimate referents are in us, the readers, but we understand what these items stand for, though meaning is only implied, because they are significantly bound to other equally well selected items, all of which are reciprocally defining. In literature, what relates concepts are story actions; the plot predicates personages and objects into statements, as verbs do literal concepts. Thus we apply the term *conclusion* to both a syllogism and a story and speak of the "logic of the events." The chaining of events in a plot corresponds to the linking of literal statements by logical conjunctions.

People project into invented stories those unobjectified forces of the psychic life that are hard to name or even recognize. At any time of life we have some inner material that we cannot express directly and explicitly; we have to say it indirectly and often unconsciously, through metaphorical fiction. Usually, the older we grow the more we can objectify and talk explicitly about feelings and ideas, but children must for a long time talk and read about these things through a sort of allegory. There are two reasons for this. One is that children are not ready to acknowledge to themselves a lot of their thoughts and feelings because they must defend against them. Another is that their abstractive powers are not developed enough to enable them to conceptualize, name, and interrelate these intangible things. As regards their deepest inner material, adults are in the same boat, and so we have art. In other words, students progressively push back the frontier of the unknown by converting the implicit into the explicit.

Whereas adults differentiate their thought into specialized kinds of discourse such as narrative, generalization, and theory, children must for a long time make narrative do for all. They utter themselves almost entirely through stories—real or invented—and they apprehend what others say through story. Young learners, that is, don't talk and read explicitly about categories and theories of experience; they talk and read about characters, events, and settings, but these are charged with symbolic meaning because they are tokens standing for unconscious classes and postulations of experience. The good and bad fairies are categories of experience, and the triumph of the good fairy is a reassuring generalization about overcoming danger. In *The Wizard of Oz* the wizard is a humbug, and the bad fairy can be destroyed by water; Dorothy is stronger than she thought, and the adults are weaker than they appear at first. *Alice in Wonderland* makes a similar statement. A tremendous amount of thought—and intricate, at that—underrides these plots. So youngsters understand that *what happened* is *what happens,* but they grow toward a differentiation of kinds of discourse to match the differentiation in abstraction levels of thought.

Growth along the fictional dimension can be described by Northrop Frye's five kinds of heroes (*Anatomy of Criticism*)—the supernatural or divine figure, the mortal but miraculous man, the king or exceptional leader, the average man, and the ironic antihero. This progressive scaling down of the hero not only traces the history of literature, with its shifts in dominant literary modes from epic and myth to legend and romance, to tragedy, to bourgeois novel and play, to a very inner and underground fiction, but it also corresponds to the withdrawal of projection, to movement from the farfetched and there-then to the actual here-now.

Children recapitulate the history of the species to this extent: they first embody their wishes for power in fantasies of omnipotence akin to the myths and epics of divine and supernatural heroes. The figures, actions, and settings they like to read about and create are as remote as possible from themselves and the circumstances of their own lives. Gradually settling for less, though, they shrink their fantasies increasingly toward figures like themselves dwelling in their own time and place, thus passing through legend and romance, tragedy, and realistic fiction. This passage comes about partly because they are gaining real power as they grow and consequently need less and less to fantasize about power, partly because they are becoming more aware of and explicit about their wishes and fears and thus want to read and write about them for what they are, and partly because they are yielding their unlimited reality to the adults' official version of reality. All this, however, does not mean that in the beginning they cannot already appreciate familiar realism in some conscious areas of experience, or that later they will not still need the farfetched modes for unconscious areas of experience.

Growth in invented stories and invented dialogue runs somewhat the reverse of growth in the literal mode. Whereas the symbolizing of recognizable, objectified experience does proceed up the ladder from the here-now to the there-then, it is in the nature of disguised psychic material that one symbolizes it first in the there-then and only gradually comes to represent it in explicitly personal terms. In other words, as regards their external observations and acknowledged feelings, people move, when speaking and writing, from the firsthand, first-person concrete levels of abstraction toward the secondhand, third-person timeless realms of abstraction. But as regards their unconscious psychic life, they move along a continuum that begins in the farfetched, with things remote from them in time and space, and work backward toward themselves. As children we project ourselves first into animals, fantastic creatures, folk heroes, and legendary figures. Slowly, the bell tolls us back to our sole self. Gradually we withdraw projection as we become willing to recognize the personal meaning symbolized in our myths, and able to objectify inner experience to the point of treating it explicitly.

**Growth Sequence 24: From there-then settings and farfetched characters and actions to the here-now of contemporary realism.**

Realistic fiction represents a return toward the literal, at least in the domain of figurative narrative. But another kind of figurative discourse may arise as narrative declines—lyric and dramatic poetry, both of which contain some of a culture's highest thought, couched in metaphor. Poetic drama tends toward the lyrical or philosophical not only in soliloquies and external monologues but even in the dialogue, which is freed from the conventions of realism by the convention of poetry itself.

The most valued poetry of a culture reaches the top of the abstraction hierarchy in *thought* but may do so in the most concrete *language.* That is, the figures make, by means of metaphor, "statements" of the most universal truth, but this truth is unparaphrasable because the depth so valued consists precisely in saying more than could ever be said in the literal mode. Great poetry breaks the bounds of language, says things it ought not to be able to say, breaches the unspeakable, which is the goal of it all.

**Growth Sequence 25: Toward poetry of increasing distillation, however concrete the language.**

The very highest growth in discourse ultimately carries a person through language entirely and back out into the wordless world, just as the story journey returns one to the here-now. If story lovers keep on growing far enough, they may realize in actuality the marvelous powers they admired in epic and supernatural figures. The final twist is that tales of power can be converted from metaphorical to literal reality. This happens at about the same stage of growth as when poetry lovers so bend language back upon itself that they spring their minds free from lifelong verbal cages and live liberated beyond thought and speech.

From all these ways of growing there results a sort of master growth that is meta-linguistic. That is, one becomes detached from language, conscious of oneself as a language user, and able to verbalize about one's verbalization. This is inseparable from becoming meta-cognitive—able to think about one's thinking. Both are major ways that consciousness itself grows, since consciousness inevitably includes forms of selfconsciousness.

With awareness of oneself as a chooser goes greater choice. "Getting on top of" discourse in this sense relates directly to familiarizing oneself with its various repertories—with the diverse kinds of discourse and the relationships among them; with the riches of vocabulary and the possibilities of sentence constructions; with all those varieties of naming, phrasing, stating, and chaining described earlier; and with the infinite creativity of how one may organize language within any particular form of discourse. Becoming familiar with *repertories* is becoming aware of *alternatives* in composing and comprehending. Alternatives are choices about how to create and interpret texts or speech acts. In this way, getting to know the pluralities of language is tantamount to raising consciousness about oneself as a chooser (if one indeed enjoys the liberty of making decisions among these alternatives). In other words, metalinguistic growth is a form of consciousness-raising, which depends not merely on grasping some concepts but on taking personal action.

**Growth Sequence 26: Toward increasing consciousness of oneself as a language user and of the language alternatives one has to choose from.**

**Figure 3**  The Forms of Thought

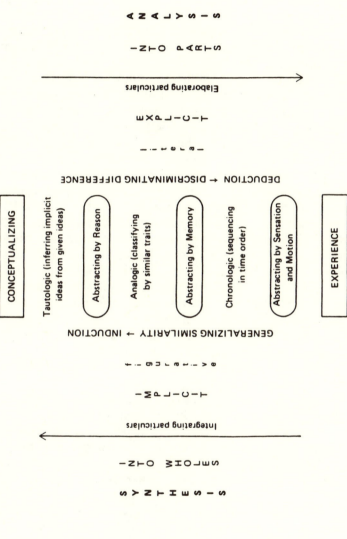

# Conclusion

To describe how people change as they grow older is to confuse inevitable and universal genetic unfolding with the relative conditioning of local culture. We do not know and may never know which changes must take place because internally programmed, and which merely depend on the time and place into which one is born. So a description of growth as known in our culture can mislead in grave ways. It can imply that some trends are good just because they happen and look like the work of nature. It can imply that some trends cannot be changed. What is biological is probably good and unchangeable except by slow evolution, but it's most likely that people's biological endowment is very open and that much of the change we see as people grow older is culturally induced. The more general, the more biological; the more specific, the more cultural, for biology governs culture as context does text.

A lot of evidence supports the idea that many changes accepted as necessary growth are cultural and that in some respects it would be better for the culture than for the child to change. Jean Piaget has said, for example, that what he regards as the highest kind of thinking prevails commonly among younger children but very little among adults—the ability to consider any state in a continuum of states as equally valid and yet to return to the point of departure. This defines *open-minded* in a way. Until about school age, children can use either brain hemisphere to process language and to do other things. Some, perhaps many, children seem to be able to see naturally the "auras" around other people (probably just certain bands of the electromagnetic spectrum) until their perception is made to conform. Many lose musical aptitude and other skills associated with the nonverbal half of the brain.

Probably the most dismal evidence of negative growth comes out of school performance itself in the form of a virtual never-failing slump starting around fourth grade, when many children suddenly don't seem to be able to read and do other things well that teachers thought they had mastered. Scores drop, attitudes become negative, and students begin dropping out either mentally or physically. It's about this time—around eight or nine years of age—that the full force of acculturation in and out of the home really hits the child. The reason this can influence growth so negatively sometimes is that culture tries to preserve itself by making everybody perceive and think and act alike, even though this ends by so starving out creativity that it dooms the culture itself.

An overemphasis of the verbal/analytic half of the brain in our own culture is endangering the culture, because it drives out the integrative, analogical thinking desperately needed to coordinate action within the vast intricacies of both individual and international life in this era of modern technology. Balance is the key, and the grand paradox is that people reason and verbalize better if they stop sometimes in favor of intuition and metaphor.

Although it is necessary to examine the problems egocentricity causes in discoursing, it would be a great mistake to regard egocentricity as just a bad thing. Failure to separate oneself from the object—not being objective—is at bottom the self's oneness with the world. It is a problem at the practical level, because getting and spending and fending and begetting all require making distinctions and then reordering the pieces of the world in some utilitarian way once you've broken it down. Jogging children out of the oneness of the world surely does them a mixed service. If it is true that for survival they simply must learn sooner or later to think and talk in analytic and linear ways, it is also true that every culture has always upheld this global feeling we call egocentricity as the basis of spirituality, and children forced out of it too soon or too far look for it again later through drugs or other ways to release their psyche from the isolating fragmentation of the analytic lesson too well learned.

The final stage of growth, though, is having the best of the mystical world of unity and the practical world of plurality—being able to play the whole abstraction scale with virtuosity and still be able in a moment to fuse self with world, one thing with another. In fact, the abstractive process carries within it the means to regain paradise. Pursuing differentiation and integration far enough leads out the other side, back into the nonverbal world. The more people interrelate the things of experience by one logic or another (including metaphor) the more they are rebuilding the world within.

Abstracting is "converting" matter to mind, a kind of alchemy. The more people at the same time make unconsciousness conscious, the more they identify with the world they are incorporating. In total fulfillment of communication's goal—to remove a differential—the inner and outer worlds equalize. This return to the newborn's unity with people and things is not, of course, mere regression. Consciousness makes the difference. The ego that arose to negotiate between the organism and the world has expanded from a point to an area. In a sense egocentricity is not at all reduced; the secret has been to expand it over the community and then over the cosmos—to overdo it extravagantly so that ego feels identified with all it encompasses by mind.

The highest abstractions cover all time and space and in fact expose time and space as mental blocks. Instead of merely projecting themselves unconsciously into what they see or read, fulfilled individuals deliberately reflect the world in their minds. Consciousness makes the difference between confusion of mind with world, and fusion of mind with world, and that difference is the most important thing a teacher needs to know about growth in language.

Other books by James Moffett available from Heinemann-Boynton/Cook

*Harmonic Learning*   0-86709-312-9   paper

*Student-Centered Language Arts, K–12*   Fourth Edition
James Moffett and Betty Jane Wagner   0-86709-292-0   paper

*Coming On Center: Essays in English Education*
Second Edition   0-86709-219-X   paper

*Teaching the Universe of Discourse*
0-86709-181-9   paper

*Active Voice: A Writing Program Across the Curriculum*
Second Edition   0-86709-289-0   paper

*Active Voices I: A Writer's Reader* (Grades 4–6)
with Marie Carducci Bolchazy and Barbara Friedberg
0-86709-091-X   cloth

*Active Voices II: A Writer's Reader* (Grades 7–9)
with Phyllis Tashlik
0-86709-111-8   paper      0-86709-205-X   cloth

*Active Voices III: A Writer's Reader* (Grades 10–12)
with Patricia Wixon, Vincent Wixon, Sheridan Blau, and John
Phreaner
0-86709-113-4   paper      0-86709-207-6   cloth

*Active Voices IV: A Writer's Reader* (College)
with Miriam Baker and Charles Cooper
0-86709-115-0   paper

For information on how to order,
call or write us at:

Heinemann-Boynton/Cook
361 Hanover Street
Portsmouth, NH 03801-3959
1-800-541-2086